Sports Fundamentals Series

BASKETBALL
Fundamentals

Jon Oliver
Eastern Illinois University

Human Kinetics

Library of Congress Cataloging-in-Publication Data

Human Kinetics Publishers.
  Basketball fundamentals / Human Kinetics with Jon Oliver.
    p. cm. -- (Sports fundamentals series)
  ISBN 0-7360-4910-X (soft cover)
  1. Basketball. I. Title. II. Series.
  GV885.O55 2003
  796.323--dc21

2003008873

ISBN: 0-7360-4910-X

Acquisitions Editor: Dean Miller; **Developmental Editor:** Cynthia McEntire; **Assistant Editor:** Scott Hawkins; **Copyeditor:** Jennifer L. Davis; **Proofreader:** Myla Smith; **Graphic Designer:** Robert Reuther; **Graphic Artist:** Tara Welsch; **Photo and Art Manager:** Dan Wendt; **Cover Designer:** Keith Blomberg; **Photographer (interior):** Dan Wendt; **Illustrator:** Roberto Sabas; **Printer:** United Graphics

Human Kinetics books are available at special discounts for bulk purchase. Special editions or book excerpts can also be created to specification. For details, contact the Special Sales Manager at Human Kinetics.

Printed in the United States of America   10 9 8 7 6 5 4 3 2

Human Kinetics
Web site: www.HumanKinetics.com

United States: Human Kinetics
P.O. Box 5076
Champaign, IL 61825-5076
800-747-4457
e-mail: humank@hkusa.com

Canada: Human Kinetics
475 Devonshire Road, Unit 100
Windsor, ON N8Y 2L5
800-465-7301 (in Canada only)
e-mail: orders@hkcanada.com

Europe: Human Kinetics
107 Bradford Road
Stanningley
Leeds LS28 6AT, United Kingdom
+44 (0)113 255 5665
e-mail: hk@hkeurope.com

Australia: Human Kinetics
57A Price Avenue
Lower Mitcham, South Australia 5062
08 8277 1555
e-mail: liaw@hkaustralia.com

New Zealand: Human Kinetics
Division of Sports Distributors NZ Ltd.
P.O. Box 300 226 Albany
North Shore City, Auckland
0064 9 448 1207
e-mail: blairc@hknewz.com

Welcome to Sports Fundamentals

The Sports Fundamentals Series uses a learn-by-doing approach to teach those who want to play, not just read. Clear, concise instructions and illustrations make it easy to become more proficient in the game or activity, allowing readers to participate quickly and have more fun.

Between the covers, this book contains rock-solid information, precise directions, and clear photos and illustrations that immerse readers in the heart of the sport. Each fundamental chapter is divided into four major sections:

- You Can Do It!: Jump right into the game or activity with a clear explanation of how to perform an essential skill or tactic.
- More to Choose and Use: Find out more about the skill or learn exciting alternatives.
- Take It to the Court: Apply the new skill in a game situation.
- Give It a Go: Use drills and game-like activities to develop skills by doing and gauge learning and performance with self-tests.

No more sitting on the sidelines! The Sports Fundamentals Series gets you right into the game. Apply the techniques and tactics as they are learned, and have fun—win or lose!

Contents

Introduction:

Preparing to Play

Basketball is one of the most popular sports in the world. Participants of all ages have discovered basketball to be fun, competitive, educational, recreational, and fitness oriented. Individual skills, such as shooting, passing, dribbling, and rebounding, along with offensive and defensive teamwork, are prerequisites for successful participation in the sport.

Although the traditional 5-on-5 game is probably the most popular basketball format, over the years a wide assortment of fun basketball-related games and competitions have evolved to help participants develop fundamental skills and knowledge. The type of game or competition played will depend on available equipment, player skill level, and number of participants. Regardless of game or competition format, basketball participation can be enriching and provide lifelong enjoyment to participants who choose to "tie up the laces" and play the game.

Beginnings

Basketball has evolved considerably since its creation in the late 19th century. Dr. James Naismith, a physical education instructor at the YMCA International Training School (now Springfield College), invented basketball in the fall of 1891. Naismith was charged by his supervisor, Luther H. Gulick, to create an indoor game to help students keep active and fit during the cold months of the Massachusetts winter. Naismith used a soccer ball and peach baskets to create the first version of the indoor game. He hung the peach baskets at a height of 10 feet and divided the class into two teams. The objective was to make, or score, more shots into the peach basket than the other team. Students immediately found this new game fun, active, and entertaining. As the game was introduced to other teachers and schools, its popularity increased and gradually spread beyond the northeastern United States.

Throughout the first half of the 20th century, new basketball leagues and associations were established to accommodate the developing interest in the sport. It was during this time period that basketball became a sanctioned sport for the National Collegiate Athletic Association (NCAA) and for the Olympic Games. Collegiate tournaments, such as the National Invitational Tournament (NIT) and the NCAA tournament, were established. By the end of the 1940s, a unified men's professional league was formed when two struggling professional leagues joined forces to create the National Basketball Association (NBA). The NBA provided an ultimate destination for skilled basketball players, but catered only to male basketball participants.

During the second half of the 20th century, basketball participation and popularity continued to boom in the United States and internationally. Professional leagues were established in various nations throughout the world, and competition gradually became more fierce at the Olympics. In the United States, federal legislation (Title IX) provided women with more opportunities to compete in interscholastic and intercollegiate athletics, leading to a huge increase in basketball participation by females. By the late 1990s, two women's professional basketball leagues (ABL and WNBA) had been established. The sport continued to receive ever-increasing media coverage and exposure via print and electronic media outlets. By the year 2000, basketball had arguably become the most popular sport in the world, with devoted fans and participants across the globe.

Key Events in the Evolution of Basketball

1891—Basketball is invented by Dr. James Naismith of the YMCA (Springfield College).

1892—Dr. Naismith develops and publishes the first official set of basketball rules.

1896—The University of Iowa and the University of Chicago play the first college basketball game.

1936—Basketball becomes an Olympic sport.

1938—The first NIT tournament is held (won by Temple University).

1939—The first NCAA tournament is held (won by the University of Oregon).

1949—The NBA is formed when two struggling professional basketball leagues merge.

1972—Title IX legislation is passed in the United States, providing women with more opportunities to compete in interscholastic and intercollegiate athletics, such as basketball.

1976—The NBA and ABA, the two main professional basketball leagues for men in the United States, merge into one league (NBA).

1985—The NCAA adopts the shot clock and the three-point line (19 feet, 9 inches).

1992—NBA players are allowed to represent the United States in the Olympic Games for the first time. The "Dream Team" easily defeats all competitors to win the gold medal.

1996—The American Basketball League (ABL), the first women's professional basketball league, begins play. It files for bankruptcy and folds in 1999.

1997—The Women's National Basketball Association (WNBA) begins play. The league is financially supported by the NBA, and eventually puts the ABL out of business.

Basic Rules

During a regulation basketball game, each team has five players on the court. Three points are awarded for each field goal made beyond the three-point line, two points are awarded for each field goal made inside the three-point line, and one point is awarded for each made free throw. A game is divided into quarters of 8 to 12 minutes each or halves of 20 minutes each. Each player is allowed up to five fouls (players in the NBA are allowed six fouls because of the longer game and more physical style of play). If a player is fouled in the act of shooting, the shooter is awarded two free throws (or three if shooting a 3-pointer).

The ball can be advanced toward the opponent's basket by dribbling or passing. If a player stops dribbling and then dribbles again (double dribble), or has stopped dribbling and takes more than one step before passing or shooting (traveling), a violation is called, and ball possession is given to the other team. The offense has a set amount of time to advance the basketball past the half-court line. Offensive players cannot position themselves within the three-second lane for more than three seconds at a time (three-second violation). A set amount of time is designated to attempt a shot (shot clock) or else possession of the basketball is given to the other team.

Defensive players can use any type of defense they wish (man-to-man, zone, combination, press, trapping, etc.) to attempt to gain possession of the basketball from the offensive team. Each team has a specific number of timeouts to use during a game. Timeouts can be used to set up a play, take a quick breather, attempt to "ice" a free-throw shooter during a close game, or diffuse a scoring run by the opponent by stopping their momentum.

All participants—players, coaches, and fans—must comply with game rules and behavioral guidelines established by the governing basketball league or association or risk being ejected from the game by the game officials. Two to three certified, trained officials oversee each game.

Equipment and Court Dimensions

Players should wear supportive, cushioned athletic shoes appropriate for the dynamic movements required by the game. They should wear nonrestrictive athletic clothing certified by the sponsoring league or association (uniform shorts, jerseys, athletic supporters, supportive bras, socks, etc.) appropriate for typical game movement and activity.

A court with baskets and an inflated ball appropriate for the court surface, either a rubber/synthetic ball for an outdoor court or a leather ball for an indoor court, are necessary. The court should be a restricted area approximately 90 feet long by 50 feet wide. The basketball goal should be 10 feet high. A three-point line appropriate for the league or association (19 feet 9 inches for high school and college, 22 feet to 23 feet 9 inches for NBA play) should be clearly marked. The free throw line is 15 feet away from the basket. The three-second lane is 12 feet wide.

Sportsmanship

The key to enjoying any basketball experience is for all participants to promote sportsmanship throughout the game. Sportsmanship is difficult to define, but is directly related to how basketball participants play by the rules, respect their opponents and the game officials, and represent themselves and their teams on the court. An enjoyable basketball game or competition can quickly turn sour if one or more participants behaves in an unsportsmanlike manner, using profane language or gestures to disrespect or disagree with an opponent or game official.

Do not waste mental and physical energy on unsportsmanlike conduct—such as trash-talking, fighting, or disputing questionable calls by the officials—when playing the game. Focus your energy toward participating at the highest skill level possible while demonstrating the best competitive attitude. If you follow these simple steps, you will never leave the basketball court angry, cheated, or unfulfilled. Whether you win or lose, you will leave knowing that you did your best, and that through additional practice and hard work, you will be able to improve your performance in the future.

Key to Diagrams

Path of dribble

Player movement, no dribble

Pass

Shot

Screen

C   Coach

X   Defensive player

Offensive player

Offensive player with the ball

1   Point guard

2   Shooting guard

3   Small forward

4   Power forward

5   Center

W   Wing

PP   Post player

P   Point

R   Rebounder

S   Shooter

O   Outlet

T   Trailer

Offensive Moves

The triple-threat position is the fundamental athletic position or stance that skilled offensive players use every time they receive the basketball, especially on the perimeter. From this position, offensive players can easily shoot, pass, or dribble. Effective use of the triple-threat position helps offensive players create individual scoring opportunities for themselves as well as for their teammates.

Michael Jordan, basketball's greatest perimeter scorer, mastered the options of the triple-threat position. By doing so, he became an unstoppable offensive force, one with the ability to create innumerable high-percentage scoring opportunities for himself and his teammates. As an offensive force, he became one of the highest per-game scorers in the history of the National Basketball Association (NBA) and a six-time NBA champion.

Body Position

The triple-threat position (figure 1.1) is easy to use. It is a basic ready, or athletic, stance that promotes a smooth transition into a quick, physical movement by the offensive player with possession of the basketball. From this athletic stance, an offensive player can immediately shoot, pass, or dribble without having to reposition the ball or make any additional body movements or adjustments.

1.1 **Triple-threat position.**

To get into the triple-threat position, stand with your feet slightly staggered, your weight on the balls of your feet. Your feet should be shoulder-width apart, toes pointing toward the basket. Knees are flexed or bent and you are leaning forward slightly at the waist. Flex your shooting arm in an L shape and load your shooting wrist and hand. The basketball is on the finger pads of the shooting hand and shoulders are square to the basket. Head is steady and square to the basket; eyes are on the basket.

For Michael Jordan, effective use of the triple-threat position often resulted in his strongly taking the basketball to the basket and dunking with authority. For the average basketball player, effective use of the triple-threat position may not result in MJ-quality dunks, but it may help in the development of higher-percentage shots, better passing lanes to teammates, and less-obstructed dribble-drive lanes to the basket.

Although the triple-threat position is ideal to use when an offensive player receives the basketball on the perimeter, establishing effective post position (figure 1.2) is a fundamental individual offensive skill that helps players receive the ball close to the basket, and leads to high-percentage scoring opportunities.

To establish post position, move toward the block, a marker painted on both sides of the three-second lane area. As you approach the block, choose a pivot foot and pivot on that foot so that your back is turned toward the basket (figure 1.2a). Bend your knees and assume a low, crouched position. If a defender is guarding you, lean your buttocks and lower back into the defender to establish a strong, solid post position. Raise a hand as a passing target toward your teammate with the basketball (figure 1.2b). This indicates to your teammate where you want an entry pass to be thrown.

1.2 **a. Back to the basket.** **b. Raise your hand.**

Michael Jordan did not create all his offensive opportunities by using only the basic ready position of the triple-threat. He had to incorporate the timely use of other individual offense fundamentals—such as jab steps, ball fakes, jump-stops, pivots, and crossover moves—to create space between himself and the defense. If MJ could get the defender off balance and create the necessary space, he could shoot, pass, or dribble to the highest-percentage shot possible.

Jab Step   The jab step (figure 1.3) is an individual offensive tactic commonly used to create space between an offensive player and a defensive player. To perform a jab step with your right foot, first assume the triple-threat position. Take a short, quick step with your right foot directly toward the defender. As you step toward the defender, move the basketball from the initial triple-threat position to a more protected position behind your body. Correct use of the jab step should cause the defender to move or retreat slightly, creating space between the two of you.

1.3   Jab step.

Crossover Move   The crossover move (figure 1.4) is commonly used to cause a defender to move or retreat in one direction so that the offensive player can quickly change directions, usually toward the basket. To perform a crossover move, assume the triple-threat position with a basketball. Use a jab step toward either side of the defender. If the jab step causes the defender to move or retreat slightly in the direction you stepped, follow it with a quick crossover step, using the same foot, to the other side of the defender. (Accompany the crossover step with a quick dribble before your stationary foot leaves the ground or you will be called for traveling.) Continue to aggressively dribble-drive in this direction to the basket for a lay-up or to an open area on the court for a perimeter jump shot.

Crossover

1.4   a. Jab step.   b. Crossover step.

Ball Fake A ball fake is used to cause a defender to move or jump off the ground. Shot fakes and pass fakes are two common types of ball fakes used in basketball. If the defender does move or jump off the ground because of the ball fake, it may create a lane or opening for the offensive player to take advantage of. To perform a shot fake (figure 1.5), assume the triple-threat position with the basketball. Quickly motion upward with the basketball and your head, as if you were beginning to attempt a jump shot. Try to sell the fake to the defender—be quick and convincing—with minimal movement. If the shot fake causes the defender to move or jump off the ground, immediately dribble-drive toward the basket or an open area of the court.

Shot Fake

 1.5   a. Step forward.   b. Fake the shot.

Jump-Stop   A jump-stop (figure 1.6) is a strong, controlled, two-footed stop that may help an offensive player establish a pivot foot, avoid traveling, or maintain good body balance. To perform a jump-stop, start in the triple-threat position and dribble the basketball from the three-point line toward the basket. As you approach the basket, simultaneously stop dribbling and bring both feet forward to a stopping point on the court. While the feet are moving toward the stopping point, position the ball between both hands. When your feet touch the ground they should be parallel to each other, and your body weight should be balanced between both feet. Don't allow your body weight to drive you forward to an off-balance position. You can now pivot on either foot. Depending on your distance from the basket, you could also immediately elevate for a jump shot or power lay-up.

Jump-Stop

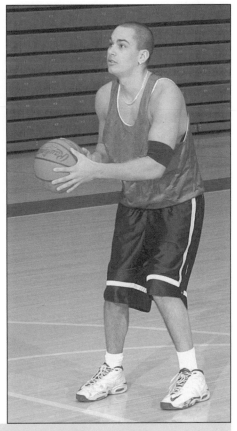

1.6   **a. Jump forward.**   **b. Land with feet parallel.**

Pivot   The use of one foot as a pivot foot (figure 1.7) allows offensive players to turn to the left or right in order to produce different offensive looks at the basket. To establish a pivot foot, first use a jump-stop, getting into a two-footed position. Next, choose which foot you will use as the pivot foot; in figure 1.7, the left foot is the pivot foot. Keep the chosen foot on the ground and use it to turn or pivot to the left or right. The pivot can improve your shooting angle to the basket or your passing angle to a teammate or can help you shield the ball from a defender.

Pivoting

| 1.7 | a. Choose a pivot foot. | b. Rotate on pivot foot. |

Reading the Defense

In a typical game situation, use the triple-threat position every time you receive the ball on the perimeter. The use of a screen or cut will help you get to an open area on the court to receive the basketball. As soon as you receive the basketball, turn or pivot to face the basket and see the defense. Read the defender by looking at his or her body and feet positions and identifying the amount of space between you and the defender. Can you spot a weak area to take advantage of? For example, is the defender off-balance or leaning? Is the defender positioned directly in front of you, or slightly off to one side? Does the defender have either foot (left or right) positioned more forward than the other? Is the defender standing upright rather than in the defensive stance? Is the defender focused on you, or more on the basketball and maybe susceptible to a ball fake?

Once you've read the defense, the effective use of one of the triple-threat options, or several of them, should create a scoring opportunity for you or a teammate. For example, imagine that when you receive the ball you see that the defense is more than one arm's length away. You should immediately attack the defense by taking the open jump shot. If the defense is playing overly aggressive (within one arm's length), you should initially attack the defender using a jab step or shot fake. This may cause the defender to jump, move, or retreat, which may produce an opportunity to dribble-drive to the basket or an open spot on the court for a jump shot. Finally, if the defender's left foot is forward, you should dribble-drive to the right because the defender will have to first use a drop-step with the left foot to initiate movement.

CATCH INTO TRIPLE-THREAT POSITION

In an open space on the court, put backspin on the basketball so that after it bounces on the ground, it moves back toward you. Catch the ball and immediately assume the triple-threat position. Add triple-threat practice options after you catch the ball, such as a shot fake; a shot fake with a dribble-drive; a shot fake with a dribble-drive plus a lay-up; a shot fake with a dribble-drive, a jump-stop, then a power lay-up; a jab step; a jab step followed by a jump shot; a jab step followed by a shot fake followed by a dribble-drive (rocker step); or a jab step followed by a crossover move with a dribble drive. Practice all of these options individually, and create other combinations that may prove to be effective in a game situation.

Instead of putting backspin on the ball by bouncing it off the court, you can pass the ball off a wall and then catch it before getting into triple-threat position. After receiving the ball, practice the individual offense fundamentals as previously described.

PASS, CATCH, AND TRIPLE-THREAT

You need a partner and a basketball for this drill. Position yourself approximately 10 feet from your partner. Pass the ball to your partner on the perimeter and assume the triple-threat position each time you receive the ball. Once you feel comfortable with the triple-threat position, have your partner play defense after passing the ball to you. Practice different individual offensive options (see the list in the Catch Into Triple-Threat Position drill) against the defender. Try to read the defense your partner is playing to identify any weaknesses that you can exploit.

If you have two partners, have one serve as an official passer while the other plays defense. The defender should play aggressively so that the offensive player has to work hard to receive the pass from the official passer. Once the pass is received, the offensive player immediately assumes the triple-threat position and reads the defense to identify any weaknesses that can be taken advantage of.

ESTABLISH POST POSITION

You need two partners for this drill. One player is the official passer, one is the defender, and one is the offensive player who tries to establish post position. The offensive player tries to establish post position as the defender works against it, and the official passer tries to pass the ball to the target hand of the post player.

ONE-ON-ONE INDIVIDUAL OFFENSE TOURNAMENT

Divide the class into equal-sized groups (three to four players per group) and assign each group to a basket. (The instructor may want to arrange the groups as players of similar skill levels.) Players compete in a one-on-one format while trying to score baskets. Emphasize the use of the triple-threat position by the offensive player after the defender checks the ball. The player who scores first stays on the court as the next defender. Players waiting to rotate in should practice the Catch Into Triple-Threat Position drill while waiting their turn. For variety, the instructor may want to rotate players to other baskets every three to five minutes.

TECHNIQUE CHECKLISTS

Technique checklists can help you check for skill development on triple-threat position technique or successful demonstration of some individual triple-threat position options.

Triple-Threat Position Technique

_____ Feet slightly staggered, weight on the balls of the feet

_____ Feet shoulder-width apart, toes pointing to the basket

_____ Knees bent, body leaning slightly forward at the waist

_____ Shooting arm flexed in an L shape, shooting wrist and hand loaded

_____ Basketball on the finger pads of the shooting hand

_____ Shoulders square to the basket

_____ Head steady, eyes on basket and defense

Triple-Threat Options

_____ Jab step

_____ Jab step and jump shot

_____ Shot fake and dribble-drive

_____ Jab step and crossover step

_____ Jab step, shot fake, and dribble-drive

_____ Dribble-drive, jump-stop, and shot fake

Inside Shots

Even with the advent of the three-point shot, a longtime basket-ball principle still applies to shooting today: the closer you are to the basket, the greater your chance of making a shot. Statistics don't lie. Although many basketball players consistently try to hit the three-point shot, statistics reveal that even the best three-point shooters make only 40 to 45 percent of their three-point attempts. The highest-percentage shots in basketball are inside shots, such as lay-ups, attempted by an offensive player positioned within a few feet of the basket.

Basketball players who take the majority of their shots close to the basket usually have the highest shooting accuracy (field goal percentage), making 55 to 60 percent of their shot attempts. For example, most of the shots Shaquille O'Neal attempts are within 10 feet of the basket, including numerous lay-ups, jump-hook shots, and monster dunks. Because he attempts and makes a high number of inside shots, it is no surprise that Shaq is usually among the NBA's leaders in field goal percentage. In fact, during the 2001-2002 NBA season, Shaquille O'Neal led the NBA in field goal percentage at 58 percent.

The Lay-Up

Although a lay-up (figure 2.1) may be the most easily made shot in basketball, the shot is not a given. Many lay-ups are missed during the course of a typical basketball game. Successfully making a lay-up still requires the use of proper technique and footwork to maximize the shot. Lay-ups can be attempted with or without the use of the backboard. However, when a player approaches the basket on either side of the basket, appropriate use of the backboard will increase the likelihood of making the shot.

To attempt a right-handed lay-up, position yourself one step away from the basket on the right-hand side of the rim. Position your right arm high and flex the shooting arm to a 90-degree angle so that it forms an L shape. Position the basketball on the finger pads of your right hand. Use the nonshooting hand to support the basketball,

2.1　　**a. Step toward the basket.**　　　　　**b. Push off the floor.**

and the nonshooting arm and elbow to provide protection from a defender who is challenging the shot. Take a step toward the basket using the left foot (figure 2.1a), then elevate off (push off) the ground using the left foot (figure 2.1b).

As you elevate off your left foot, extend your right arm toward the target point on the backboard (figure 2.1c). Softly release the basketball out of the shooting hand toward the target point so that the ball doesn't bounce off the backboard too strongly (figure 2.1d). Maintain eye contact with the target point until after the ball contacts the backboard and goes in the basket.

Reverse the directions to attempt a lay-up from the left side of the basket (shoot with the left hand, elevate off the ground using the right foot).

c. Elevate and extend.

d. Release and follow through.

The target point for a right-handed lay-up is the top-right corner of the backboard square (figure 2.2). The backboard square is immediately above the back of the rim on most standard backboards.

Offensive players frequently use other types of inside shots when they are positioned close to the basket. Reverse lay-ups, power lay-ups, hook shots, and jump-hook shots are alternatives to the traditional lay-up. These shots can be used when an offensive player has a scoring opportunity close to the basket but the defense doesn't allow a traditional lay-up attempt.

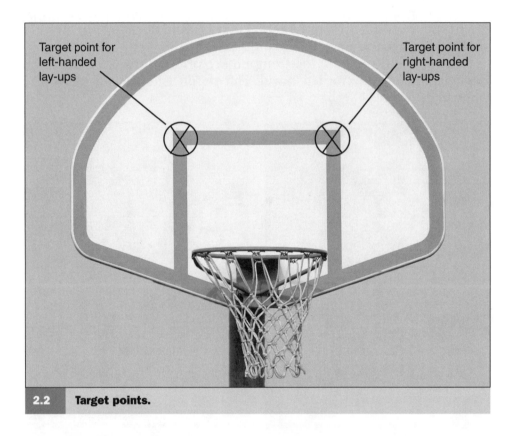

Target point for left-handed lay-ups

Target point for right-handed lay-ups

2.2 **Target points.**

Reverse Lay-Up A reverse lay-up (figure 2.3) is an inside shot that is commonly used when an offensive player is underneath the basket or positioned too close to the basket to attempt a regular lay-up. A reverse lay-up is also commonly used when an offensive player dribble-drives to the basket and wants to use the basket as a shield against a challenging defender. The technique for the reverse lay-up is similar to that of a regular lay-up. The main differences are that the shooter uses the opposite side of the backboard for the reverse lay-up and will probably not have as good a view of the target point on the backboard when attempting a reverse lay-up.

For a right-handed reverse lay-up, position the basketball on the finger pads of your right hand. Take a step with the left foot and elevate off the left foot as you move underneath the rim (figure 2.3a). Extend the right arm toward the other side of the basket as you begin to elevate toward the rim. As your body moves to the other side of the rim, use soft hands and a wrist snap to flip the ball out of the shooting hand toward an estimated target point on the backboard (figure 2.3b). Be gentle so that the ball doesn't bounce off the backboard too strongly. Try to maintain eye contact with the backboard until after the shot is released and the ball goes in the basket. Use the nonshooting hand to support the basketball and the nonshooting

2.3   **a. Move under the basket.**   **b. Reverse lay-up.**

2.4 **Power lay-up.**

arm and elbow to protect against defenders. The rim will also serve as a shield against a defensive player trying to block the shot. A successfully executed reverse lay-up is impressive to watch because it typically requires a high level of ball and body control to successfully complete.

Power Lay-Up A power lay-up (figure 2.4) is often used when an offensive player positioned close to the basket receives a pass, gains possession of the basketball from a rebound, or makes a jump-stop after a dribble-drive to the basket. Usually defenders who are close by try to reach in to steal or block the ball, so strong hands are needed to maintain possession of the ball while attempting the power lay-up.

For a power lay-up on the right side of the basket, position the ball firmly between both hands. Elevate strongly off the ground using both feet. As you elevate, extend your arms toward the rim and backboard so that the ball is held in a high position. As you reach the peak of your jump, smoothly transfer the ball from both hands into the finger pads of your shooting hand, using your nonshooting arm and elbow as protection against defenders. At the peak of your elevation, use soft hands as you release the basketball from your shooting hand toward the target point on the backboard. Be gentle so that the ball doesn't bounce off the backboard too strongly. Maintain eye contact with the target point until after the ball touches the backboard and goes in the basket. If you miss the power lay-up, you should be in a good position to get the offensive rebound, so jump strongly after landing to regain possession of the ball.

2.5 **Hook shot.**

Hook Shot   Post players who have their backs turned to the basket frequently use a hook shot (figure 2.5). Hook shots are difficult to defend or block and can be very effective against taller players. The hook shot is often used when an offensive player receives the basketball close to the basket but not close enough to use a lay-up, reverse lay-up, or power lay-up. Some of the basic footwork used for shooting lay-ups is useful when shooting hook shots.

To attempt a right-handed hook shot, position yourself a few steps away from the basket with your back fully turned to the basket. Position your right arm in the L position, similar to the shooting position used for lay-ups. Place the ball on the finger pads of your right hand. Take a step to the left with your left foot and then elevate off the ground using your left foot. Drive your right knee up and rotate your shoulders and head toward the basket. As you elevate, gradually extend your right arm so that the ball is held high. Use your nonshooting arm and elbow as protection against defenders. Gently snap your right wrist toward the basket and allow the ball to roll off your fingertips toward the rim. After the release of the ball, use a follow-through motion toward the basket with your right hand and fingers. Maintain eye contact with the rim until after the shot is released and the ball goes in the basket. Your hook shot will be very difficult to block if your shooting arm is held high and away from defenders.

Jump-Hook Shot   A jump-hook (figure 2.6) is a variation of a hook shot that doesn't require the use of a step before the shot. Similar to a hook shot, a jump-hook can be an effective offensive weapon, and is difficult to defend against or block.

To attempt a right-handed jump-hook, position yourself a few steps from the basket with your back turned toward the basket. Position your right arm in the L position and place the ball on the finger pads of your right hand. Partially turn your head and shoulders so that you can see the basket. Slightly pivot to the left on your left foot to help you better see the basket. Elevate using both feet. As you elevate, extend your

2.6   Jump-hook shot.

right arm so that the ball is held high. Use your nonshooting arm and elbow as protection against defenders. Gently snap your right wrist toward the basket and allow the ball to roll off your fingertips toward the rim. After releasing the ball, use a follow-through motion toward the basket with your right hand and fingers. Maintain eye contact with the rim until after the shot is released and the ball goes in the basket. A jump-hook shot is very difficult to block if the shooting arm is held high and away from defenders.

Take it to the court

Scoring Inside

Because a lay-up may be the highest-percentage shot in basketball, offensive players should try to perform as many lay-ups as possible during each game. Individual players and teams must develop a mind-set that producing lay-ups is a top priority when playing offense. Offensive teammates need to do the little things on offense, such as setting screens for each other, cutting to open areas close to the basket, and making precise passes to teammates, in order to create as many lay-up opportunities as possible.

Various game situations where lay-ups and other inside shots are typically used include when a player cuts to the basket (e.g., the curl cut or backdoor cut) and receives a pass from a teammate; when a player uses a strong dribble-drive to advance the ball to the basket; when a player involved in a fast break receives the ball close to the basket and finishes the fast break; when a player establishes post position close to the basket and receives a pass from a teammate; and when a player gets an offensive rebound close to the basket and immediately shoots a second-chance shot. In each of these situations, the offensive player should remember to elevate off the ground using the correct foot, use the correct shooting hand, use the nonshooting hand to support the basketball, use the nonshooting arm and elbow to protect the basketball when a defender is challenging the shot, go up strongly and anticipate body contact when a defender is challenging (this may result in a defensive foul, generating two free throws for the offensive player), and use the target point on the backboard to maximize shooting success.

A few game situations may not warrant the use of the backboard with an inside shot, including times when an offensive player approaches the basket from the baseline or when an offensive player approaches the basket from the middle of the lane. Neither of these situations provides the offensive player with a good angle or view of the target point on the backboard. However, players should try to approach the basket using a good angle so that the target point on the backboard is in full view and usable for the inside shot whenever possible.

ONE-STEP LAY-UP

Start one step away from the basket to either the left or right of the basket. Take one step toward the basket using the proper foot and shooting mechanics to attempt 10 right-handed lay-ups, then 10 left-handed lay-ups. If you make 10 shots out of 10 attempts, you are a hall-of-famer. If you make 9 of 10, you are an MVP. If you make 8 of 10, consider yourself an all-star. If you make 6 to 7 out of 10, you're a starter, but if you make less than 6 out of 10 attempts, just keep practicing!

If you made more than half of your lay-ups, take another step back from the basket. Your starting point is now two steps away from the basket. Take two steps and, using the proper foot and shooting techniques, attempt 10 right-handed lay-ups and 10 left-handed lay-ups. Use the same scoring system to analyze your performance.

For variety, try these alternatives:

- Three-step lay-ups (left-handed and right-handed)
- Dribble-drive from the free-throw line to a lay-up (both sides of the basket)
- Dribble from the free-throw line, make a jump-stop, and complete a power lay-up
- Tap the ball off the backboard, make an offensive rebound, and complete a power lay-up

FREE-THROW LINE LAY-UPS WITH DEFENSE

Divide participants into partners. The player with the basketball (offense) stands on the court at either one of the free-throw line elbows. The other player (defense) stands just inside the three-second lane close to the spot where the offensive player will elevate for a lay-up. The offensive player dribbles toward the basket and attempts five lay-ups on each side of the basket (figure 2.7). The defensive player stands in the designated position with one arm extended high in order to challenge each lay-up attempt. The defensive player gradually increases defensive intensity.

FULL-COURT LAY-UPS

Divide the class into two to four groups, depending on the number of full basketball courts available. Each group should have an approximately equal number of participants and one basketball. Position each group in a single-file line behind the baseline of op-

2.7 Lay-ups with a challenge.

posing baskets. At the sound of a whistle, the first player in each line dribbles the length of the court with the right hand and shoots a right-handed lay-up at the basket where the opposite team is positioned (figure 2.8). Once the player makes the right-handed lay-up, he or she dribbles the ball back to the other basket using the left hand and shoots a left-handed lay-up. Once the player makes the left-handed lay-up, he or she hands the ball off to the next teammate in line. All players follow the same guidelines for dribbling and shooting lay-ups. The first team to have all members make their lay-ups wins.

HALF-COURT 3-ON-3, 4-ON-4, OR 5-ON-5 WITH INSIDE SHOTS

Divide the class into teams of three, four, or five players, depending on the total number of participants. Assign two teams

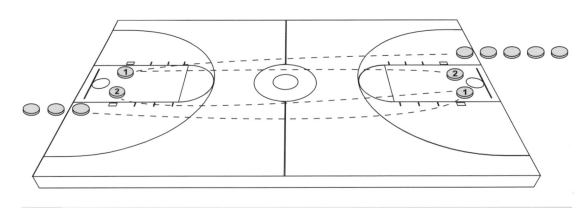

2.8 Full-court lay-ups setup.

to each basket. The teams will play a half-court basketball game. The only shots that can be taken during the game are inside shots, such as lay-ups, power lay-ups, hook shots, or jump-hook shots within the three-second lane. If a team accidentally uses a type of shot other than those specified, a quick freeze in the action occurs, and all team members must immediately complete a simple conditioning task, such as five knee-highs, jumping jacks, pushups, or a similar conditioning activity. Play three- to five-minute games and then rotate teams.

TECHNIQUE CHECKLISTS

Technique checklists can help you check for skill development in lay-up technique or other inside shots.

Lay-Up Technique Checklist

_____ Shooting arm is held high in L shape

_____ Ball is on the finger pads of the shooting hand

_____ Player steps with the correct foot and elevates off the correct foot

_____ Player extends the shooting arm toward the target point on the backboard

_____ Player uses the nonshooting hand and arm to support and protect the ball

_____ The ball contacts the target point on the backboard

_____ The lay-up attempt is successful

General Inside Shot Checklist

_____ Lay-up (right-handed and left-handed)

_____ Reverse lay-up (right-handed and left-handed)

_____ Power lay-up (both sides of the basket)

_____ Hook shot

_____ Jump-hook shot

Outside Shots

Every basketball player has the potential to become a skilled perimeter shooter. Observe talented outside shooters and you will notice that each player utilizes comparable fundamentals when shooting a basketball. Many of the basic shooting fundamentals used for outside shots can be directly applied to both the jump shot and the free throw. Therefore, it is no coincidence that accurate jump shooters are typically accurate free-throw shooters.

Reggie Miller has established himself as one of the all-time great perimeter shooters in the history of basketball, delivering a number of amazing shooting performances throughout his collegiate and professional careers. Reggie has made a significant impression on the NBA record books through the consistent use of sound shooting fundamentals. Reggie currently ranks as the NBA's all-time leader in three-point shots made. In addition, he has always been one of the most accurate free-throw shooters in the NBA, leading the league in free-throw shooting percentage during the 2001-2002 season and ranking 6th all-time in NBA free-throw shooting percentage.

The Perimeter Shot

Accurate perimeter shooters use a consistent arm, ball, and body position with each outside shot they attempt. Each shot is initiated from a shooting pocket—a basic ready shooting position that uses similar biomechanics to the triple-threat position discussed in chapter 1.

Establishing an effective shooting position (shooting pocket) begins with the correct body position. Stand with feet slightly staggered, shoulder-width apart, weight on the balls of your feet, toes pointed toward the basket, with knees flexed or bent, and body slightly leaning forward at the waist. This is a good ready position for receiving a pass, as shown in figure 3.1a, and for loading up to take the perimeter shot after receiving a pass or after dribbling up court.

Flex the shooting arm in an L shape (figure 3.1b), forming a 90-degree angle at the elbow. Place the shooting hand and wrist in a flat position, and position the shooting hand above the right shoulder (for a right-handed shooter).

The ball position is also important. Place the basketball on the finger pads of the shooting hand. Position the nonshooting hand on the side of the basketball to guide and support the ball. Point feet toward the basket, and align the shoulders and head so that they are square with the basket.

Execute and finish the shot (figure 3.1c), using a wrist snap and a proper follow-through. Be prepared to follow your shoot for a rebound if the ball doesn't go in the basket.

Good perimeter shooters have confidence in their shooting ability, but they also realize that they probably won't make more than 50 percent

3.1   **a. Establishing shooting pocket position.**

of the shots they attempt. Therefore, following a shot to the basket for a potential offensive rebounding opportunity is another important fundamental that perimeter shooters must practice and master. More than any other player on the court, the shooter has the most accurate idea of whether a shot will go in the basket. As soon as the shooter realizes that an attempted shot will miss, he or she should immediately move toward the basket, establish offensive rebounding position, and aggressively pursue the offensive rebound.

b. Good shooting-arm position.

c. Wrist snap and follow-through.

Making a Jump Shot   Elevate off the court by flexing the knees, pushing off with the feet, and extending the legs (figure 3.2a). At the peak of elevation, snap the shooting wrist and hand directly toward the rim. The wrist snap will apply backspin to the ball as it rolls off the finger pads toward the target. Apply a high shooting arc to the ball. Emphasize the follow-through by holding the finishing position of the shooting hand, wrist, and arm until the ball reaches the basket (figure 3.2b).

Jump Shot

3.2   a. Elevate.   b. Snap the wrist.

Making a Free Throw Use the leg muscles to extend the knees, generating the necessary force for the shot (figure 3.3a). As the knees become fully extended, snap the shooting wrist and hand toward the basket (figure 3.3b). The wrist snap will apply backspin to the ball as it rolls off the finger pads toward the target. Emphasize the follow-through by holding the finishing position of the shooting hand, wrist, and arm until the ball reaches the basket.

Free Throw

3.3   **a. Extend the knees.**   **b. Snap the wrist and follow through.**

With both a jump shot and a free throw, good perimeter shooters focus their eyes on the target (rim) before, during, and after the execution of the shot. After the shot is released, good shooters emphasize the follow-through by holding the shooting arm above the head in the follow-through position until the basketball reaches the target.

Successful free-throw shooters typically use a preshot routine every time they attempt free throws in practice or game situations. A preshot routine consists of elements that help a player physically and mentally focus on executing a smooth, fluid free throw. To establish a free-throw preshot routine, first identify simple elements or tasks that may help you focus, such as a deep breath; a cue word like "focus," "confidence," or "relax;" or a few bounces of the basketball. As you identify elements that may help you, organize them into a sequence or routine. Consistently use the sequence or routine as you practice shooting free throws. If the routine helps you relax and focus on the shooting task and improves your free-throw shooting performance in practice, try incorporating the routine into game situations. After you have used the routine in a few game situations, conduct a self-evaluation to determine if the free-throw preshot routine helped you improve your free-throw shooting performance during games.

Applying Arc   Skilled perimeter shooters apply a high arc to their shots (figure 3.4). Using a higher arc allows the ball to approach the basket at a more advantageous angle, increasing the likelihood of its clearing the front of the rim and going into the basket. A shooter doesn't have to bring rain by applying too much arc to a shot. However, a shot with minimal arc will most likely contact either the front or back of the rim and bounce strongly away from the basket.

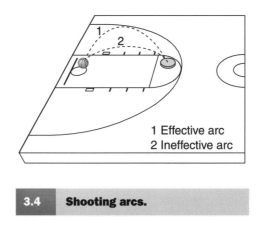

1 Effective arc
2 Ineffective arc

3.4   **Shooting arcs.**

Set Shot Versus Jump Shot

Some perimeter shooters have mastered the fundamentals of the jump shot without elevating off the ground while shooting. This is referred to as a set shot (figure 3.5), and can be a very effective method of shooting. Larry Bird, one of basketball's all-time great clutch shooters, was a master of the set shot. Larry possessed an incredibly accurate and soft shooting touch and could torch the net with his set shot from virtually anywhere on the court. Because of his quick, high release point and high shot arc, his set shots were rarely blocked, even though he often did not elevate off the court when he attempted them.

3.5 Set shot.

Take it to the court

Stop, Hop, and Shoot

Every basketball team needs skilled perimeter shooters to be successful. Good shooters add offensive firepower to a team and extend defenses, requiring the defense to play farther away from the basket than desired. As the defense extends to the perimeter to defend skilled perimeter shooters, better passing lanes are created for offensive teammates positioned close to the basket. Higher-percentage scoring opportunities are often the end result.

Consistent use of correct shooting fundamentals is the key to long-term shooting success in game situations. Game situations in which the use of an outside shot is appropriate include instances

- when a player receives the ball on the perimeter, faces the basket, and finds there is immediately enough space (more than one arm's length) between himself and the defender to successfully attempt an outside shot;

- when a player is able to use triple-threat position options, such as dribbling, to create sufficient space between him- or herself and the defender to successfully attempt a jump shot;

- when a player uses a screen from a teammate to cut to an open area on the court so that he or she can successfully receive a pass and attempt a shot (the player should use a fluid catch-n-shoot motion to attempt the perimeter shot); and

- when a player dribble-drives toward the basket, but a defender doesn't allow a lay-up to be attempted (the offensive player should use an effective jump-stop, elevate, and attempt a short jump shot).

Give it a go: Outside Shots

WRIST-SNAP FOLLOW-THROUGH

Lie on your back. Place the ball in the correct shooting pocket position. Visualize a basket (target) above your head to shoot at. Shoot the ball straight in the air, emphasizing the wrist snap, release, and follow through toward the target (figure 3.6). Try to maximize the height of the ball as you use a smooth, fluid shooting motion. This is an effective activity for building shooting strength in the hands and wrists. Attempt at least 20 consecutive repetitions with each hand.

INDIVIDUAL CATCH-N-SHOOT

Pass to yourself by using either backspin on the ball and bouncing it off the court or passing the ball off a wall so that it bounces back into your hands. Catch the ball, immediately align your feet, head, and shoulders to the basket, elevate off the court, and shoot the ball, emphasizing a high follow-though position with the shooting hand. This is an effective activity for practicing the quick catch-n-shoot motion.

3.6 **Wrist-snap follow-through drill.**

Gradually add a combination of triple-threat options to your shooting practice immediately after catching the ball, such as a shot fake; one dribble and shoot; or a jump-stop, shot fake, and shot. Practice from different spots on the court.

PARTNER CATCH-N-SHOOT

Have a partner feed you passes at different spots on the court. Square your feet and shoulders to the basket before the ball arrives, catch the ball, elevate off the court, and shoot the ball, emphasizing a high arc and the follow-through position of the shooting hand.

After practicing the catch-n-shoot for a while, have your partner play defense after you catch the ball, gradually progressing from initially extending a hand toward you as you shoot the ball to playing aggressive man-to-man defense to make the practice activity more gamelike.

HOT-SPOTS SHOOTING COMPETITION

Assign point values for made baskets at different spots on the court. Give each student a set time (e.g., 30 seconds) to accumulate as many points as possible while shooting from the designated spots. Use a scoring guideline like the one shown in table 3.1 to rate student performance. Adjust scoring criteria depending on the participants' experience levels.

TABLE 3.1 HOT-SPOTS COMPETITION

Scoring criteria	30-second test	60-second test
Lay-up = 1 point	More than 15 = Hall-of-famer	More than 30 = Hall-of-famer
Free-throw line = 2 points	13 to 15 points = MVP	25 to 30 points = MVP
15-foot perimeter = 2 points	9 to 12 points = All-star	17 to 24 points = All-star
Three-point line = 3 points	5 to 8 points = Starter	9 to 16 points = Starter
	0 to 4 points = Keep practicing	0 to 8 points = Keep practicing

TECHNIQUE CHECKLIST

A technique checklist can help you check for skill development in shooting technique.

Shooting Technique Checklist: Outside Shots

_____ Correct use of the L form with the shooting arm

_____ Basketball on finger pads, wrist cocked or loaded

_____ Shooting pocket established

_____ Feet, shoulders, body facing the basket (square to the basket)

_____ Elevation off the court for the jump shot

_____ Extension of legs for the free throw

_____ Wrist snap, release, and follow-through toward the basket with the shooting hand

_____ Follow-through position held high (above head) until ball reaches the rim

---

Passing

Precise passing is one of the keys to successful team offense and a component of high-percentage shots. The value of a great pass should never be underrated. It can motivate teammates, excite spectators, and promote unselfish play. A skilled passer is able to see the whole court, anticipate the development of an offensive play, and deliver the basketball to a teammate at the right time.

John Stockton has exemplified the attributes of a great passer throughout his career in the NBA. While considerably smaller than the average NBA player at 6 feet, 1 inch, Stockton uses keen vision, court awareness, and precision passing to deliver the basketball to his teammates. John has mastered the art of passing, becoming the NBA's all-time leader in career assists by averaging over 10 assists per game throughout his career.

Chest and Bounce Passes

The two-handed chest pass is probably the most frequently used pass in the game of basketball. It is a reliable pass used to transfer the ball from one teammate to another, usually on the perimeter. The two-handed bounce pass can be used to effectively pass the ball to a teammate when you need to avoid a defender or when a direct chest pass could be easily intercepted.

To perform a chest pass, position yourself approximately 10 feet from a target, such as a partner or a gym wall. Place your hands on the sides of the basketball and gradually bend (flex) your arms so that the ball is brought close to your chest (figure 4.1a).

To initiate the pass, extend your arms toward the target (figure 4.1b). As your arms become fully extended, gradually roll the ball off your finger pads. Your fingers should end up pointing toward your target, and your thumbs should end up pointing toward the ground. This finger-thumb action will apply a little bit of backspin to the ball as it travels toward the target.

4.1 a. Chest pass: Bring the ball close to your chest.

b. Extend your arms to the target and release the ball.

Emphasize the follow-through by holding and pointing your arms directly toward the target after releasing the ball. If necessary, step toward your target with either foot to add more force to the pass.

The bounce pass (figure 4.2) is effective when you need to pass low past a defender to get the ball to a teammate. To attempt a bounce pass, use the same passing technique used with the chest pass. However, rather than pass the ball directly to your partner's hands, bounce the ball on the court approximately two-thirds of the way to your partner. After contacting the court, the ball will bounce up into your partner's hands, usually around waist height. Emphasize the follow-through by pointing your arms toward the target on the court after releasing the ball. If necessary, step toward your target with either foot when passing the ball to add more force to the pass.

4.2   **Bounce pass: Extend your arms, bouncing the ball to the target.**

Other Passes   Many other types of passes are commonly used in basketball, including the two-handed overhead pass, the baseball pass, the shuffle pass, the off-the-dribble pass, the wrap-around pass, and the behind-the-back pass. Each type of pass has specific uses in game situations. Master each type of pass to become the kind of player who makes things happen on the court.

The two-handed overhead pass (figure 4.3) is effective when you need to pass over a defender to get the ball to a teammate. To perform an overhead pass, place your hands on the sides of the ball. Position the ball behind your head. Move your arms toward the target (a partner or the gym wall), using a quick forward motion. As your arms move forward toward the target, snap your wrists and release the ball. The wrist-snap will add more strength to the pass. Emphasize the follow-through by pointing your arms and hands toward the target after releasing the ball. If necessary, step toward the target with either foot when passing the ball to add more force to the pass.

The baseball pass (figure 4.4) is effective when you need to make a long pass to get the ball to a teammate, such as when inbounding the ball with your teammate at half court. To perform a baseball pass, position the basketball in one hand, similar to the way you hold a baseball. Bring your throwing arm back behind your head. As you step toward your target, rotate your shoulders and pass the

4.3   **Overhead pass.**

4.4   **Baseball pass.**

ball toward the target using a baseball-throwing motion. Emphasize the follow-through by pointing your passing arm toward the target after releasing the ball. Be careful not to throw the ball over your target's head.

The shuffle pass (figure 4.5) is effective when you need to pass the ball to a teammate who is close to you or to a teammate who makes a cut close by you. The shuffle pass can be an effective tool in helping a teammate get around the defense to make an easy score. To perform a shuffle pass, place the ball in one hand and position it close to the body. Extend your arm toward a close target (a partner or the gym wall), allowing the ball to roll off your fingertips, and apply a gentle wrist snap (flip) toward the target just before the ball leaves your hand. The shuffle pass is almost like a quick flip or a long handoff of the basketball to a teammate.

4.5 **Shuffle pass.**

The off-the-dribble pass (figure 4.6) is effective when you need to pass the ball to a teammate directly from an active dribble. To attempt an off-the-dribble pass, begin dribbling the basketball with either hand. Identify a target (a partner or the gym wall) to pass the ball to. As the ball approaches the apex of a bounce, quickly slide your dribbling hand behind the ball and extend your dribbling arm toward the target. This pushing motion will cause the ball to travel toward the target. Use a wrist snap with the

4.6 **Pass off the dribble.**

4.7 Wrap-around pass.

passing hand to apply more force to the ball. Emphasize the follow-through by pointing your passing arm toward the target after releasing the ball.

The wrap-around pass (figure 4.7) is effective when you need to move laterally to transfer the ball past a defender to a teammate. To attempt a left-handed wrap-around pass, first place the ball in your left hand. Take a step to the left using your left foot. Gradually extend your left arm laterally to the outside of the defender. Bounce the ball on a target point on the court that is two-thirds of the way toward your partner. Use a wrist snap with the passing hand to generate more force on the pass.

4.8 Behind-the-back pass.

The ball should successfully bounce off the target point on the court into the hands of your teammate. Emphasize the follow-through by pointing your passing hand toward the target point on the court after releasing the ball.

The behind-the-back pass (figure 4.8) is effective when you want to add an element of surprise to a pass in order to get the ball past a defender to a teammate. To initiate the pass, place the ball in the passing hand. Using the passing arm and hand, swing the ball around your back and extend your passing arm toward the target. As the ball rolls off the fingertips of the passing hand, add a wrist snap to apply more force to the pass.

Catching Passes   Catching a good pass is just as important as making a good pass. The receiver must be aware of where the basketball is at all times and be prepared to receive a pass at any moment. A receiver should also create a target with his or her hands for the passer, identifying where the pass should be thrown. A receiver also must decide whether to use one or two hands to catch the ball.

To make a two-handed catch above the waist (figure 4.9a), position the hands close together, with thumbs and index fingers almost touching each other. With hands positioned close together forming a target, the ball will have little chance of passing through the fingers and going out of bounds. Use the finger pads of the hands, not the palms, to catch the ball.

To make a two-handed catch below the waist (figure 4.9b), bend your knees so that your body moves lower toward the court. Position the hands close together, with the fingers pointing toward the court and the palms up. Again, use the finger pads of the hands, not the palms, to catch the ball.

Post players often make one-handed catches when positioned close to the basket. To make a one-handed catch (figure 4.10), extend one arm away from the body with fingers spread to form a passing target for teammates. As the ball is passed to you, catch it with the finger

4.9   **a. Two-handed catch above the waist.**   **b. Two-handed catch below the waist.**

4.10 **One-handed catch.**

pads of the target hand. Immediately bring the ball in close to the body so that a defender cannot tip it away. Move the nontarget hand to the ball to secure possession before initiating an inside shot or offensive move.

Take it to the court

Making Smart Passes

Different game situations require the use of different passes. During game play, offensive players need to be able to deliver accurate passes to both stationary and moving teammates. When on offense, a team must try to create the highest-percentage shot possible by quickly passing the ball from player to player around the court. Quick, precise passes can effectively move defenders, making the defense adjust to the position of the basketball on the court. During this process, offensive opportunities will develop as offensive players exploit defensive weaknesses and distribute the ball to players positioned close to the basket.

During game situations, chest and bounce passes are commonly used by offensive players passing the ball around the perimeter, such as point-to-wing passes. Overhead passes are frequently used when a wing player swings the basketball all the way to the other side of the court, usually to another wing player. Soft overhead passes, sometimes referred to as lob passes, are often used for entry into the post area when defenders are positioned in front of post players. Bounce and wrap-around passes are frequently used for entry into the post area when defenders are positioned behind post players. In fast-break situations, a combination of chest, bounce, baseball, and off-the-dribble passes are used to move the ball quickly up the court, depending on the length of the pass required. Baseball and overhead passes are used to make longer passes in fast-break, pressing, and inbounding situations. Finally, behind-the-back passes are creative passes that are sometimes used in fast-break situations to surprise a defender.

Give it a go: Passing

PERSONAL PASS

Practice different types of passes by passing to a target point on a gym wall. Use tape or chalk to create a target on the wall. Emphasize successful catching as the ball bounces off the wall and back into your hands. Gradually move farther away from the wall to increase the challenge of each pass.

PARTNER PASS

With a partner, pass back and forth using a variety of passes. After a bit, the receiver should start to move randomly on the court so that the passer can practice passing to a moving target. Emphasize accuracy by passing directly to the receiver's target.

KEEP AWAY

Position a defensive player between two offensive players. The offensive players use a variety of passes to keep the ball away from the defender (figure 4.11). The defender should gradually increase defensive intensity. If the defender intercepts a pass, he or she switches places with the offensive player who threw the intercepted pass.

4.11   Playing keep away.

FULL-COURT PARTNER PASSING

Have the group form two lines behind one of the baselines (figure 4.12). Player lines should be approximately 8 to 10 feet away from each other (approximate width of the three-second lane). The first player in each line steps in-bounds and faces the other. At the sig-

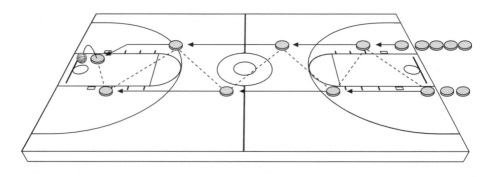

4.12   Full-court partner passing.

nal, the players begin passing a basketball back and forth to each other while moving to the other end of the court. As they approach the basket at the other end of the court, one of the players shoots a lay-up. Emphasize accurate passing to a moving target. The next two players in line begin the drill after the partners in front of them move past half-court.

STAR DRILL

At least six participants form five lines at center court in a star formation (figure 4.13). The first player in one of the lines passes across the center circle to the first player in another line. The ball should be passed from line to line, as if the ball were drawing a star on the court. To make this a continuous drill, after passing the ball, players should go to the end of the line they just passed to. Emphasize accurate passing to a stationary target.

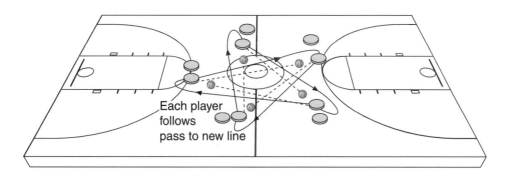

4.13 **Star drill setup.**

BIRDIE-IN-THE-CAGE/MOUSE-IN-THE-MIDDLE

Five offensive players form a circle, or cage, around one defensive player (figure 4.14). The offensive players begin passing the ball to each other while trying to keep the defender from intercepting a pass. Gradually add more defensive players to the cage to increase the passing challenge for the offensive players. If a defensive player intercepts a pass, the defender switches places with the offensive player who threw the pass.

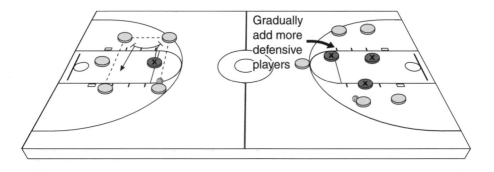

4.14   **Birdie-in-the-cage/mouse-in-the-middle setup.**

SELF-TEST: INDIVIDUAL PASSING

For this drill you can pass to a stationary target, such as a wall, or a moving target, such as a partner. For a stationary target, mark a target on a wall that is approximately chest high. Move approximately 10 feet from the wall and attempt 10 consecutive passes using each type of pass—chest, bounce, overhead, baseball, etc. For a moving target, have a partner move randomly around the court. Try to hit your partner's hands (target) with accurate passes 10 consecutive times. Use a scoring guideline like the one shown in table 4.1.

TABLE 4.1 SELF-TEST SCORING CHART

Stationary target	Moving target
Hit target 10 times = Hall-of-famer	Hit target 9 to 10 times = Hall-of-famer
Hit target 9 times = MVP	Hit target 8 times = MVP
Hit target 7 to 8 times = All-star	Hit target 7 times = All-star
Hit target 5 to 6 times = Starter	Hit target 6 times = Starter
Hit target 0 to 4 times = Keep practicing	Hit target 0 to 5 times = Keep practicing

TECHNIQUE CHECKLIST

Instructors and players can use a technique checklist to check for specific fundamentals on various passes.

Passing Checklist

_____ Chest pass: correct technique, successful pass

_____ Bounce pass: correct technique, successful pass

_____ Overhead pass: correct technique, successful pass

_____ Pass to post: correct technique, successful pass

_____ Baseball pass: correct technique, successful pass

_____ Shuffle pass: correct technique, successful pass

_____ Wrap-around pass: correct technique, successful pass

_____ Behind-the-back pass: correct technique, successful pass

_____ Off-the-dribble pass: correct technique, successful pass

Dribbling

Dribbling is one of the first basketball fundamentals introduced to beginners because of how important the skill is to each player involved in a basketball game. Every basketball participant can become a skilled dribbler because dribbling can be practiced anywhere at any time. No other players or equipment is needed: Just a basketball. But you don't progress into a dribbling phenom overnight. It takes focused practice and participation in games to develop your dribbling skills to a proficient level. You will know if you have become a talented dribbler if you can dribble a basketball with either hand, at various speeds, and in different directions without ever having to look down at the ball.

Every team needs players who have the confidence and skill to dribble the basketball against any type of defense. Isiah Thomas, former point guard for the Detroit Pistons, was known for his dribbling abilities during his playing career. Commonly shredding the defense on his way to the basket, Isiah was proficient with many dribbling moves and equally skilled with either hand. He developed into a floor general on the court and led the Pistons to two NBA championships before he retired.

Ball Control

Dribbling prowess develops as you practice bouncing and dribbling different kinds of balls. This kind of focused practice creates a keen sense of where the ball is without the players having to look down at the ball. The dribbler is able to keep his or her eyes up, surveying the positions of defenders and teammates.

A skilled dribbler can dribble with either hand, at different speeds, while keeping the eyes up. A proficient dribbler can dribble in different directions depending on the game situation and the position of defenders. In addition, skilled dribblers are able to avoid violations such as double dribbling, traveling, or palming.

Although dribbling might be one of the first basketball skills that players are introduced to, it takes consistent practice using correct fundamentals to develop into a proficient dribbler. Basketball participants should focus on the following fundamentals to develop their dribbling skills (see figure 5.1):

5.1   **a. Use your fingers.**   **b. Dribble with control.**

Keep your head up. Use your eyes and peripheral vision to see the court and your teammates. Develop a feel for the ball. Trust your hands. Don't look down at the basketball. Stay aware of where the defenders are and where your teammates are so you can take advantage of a scoring opportunity that opens up, or to pass the ball if the defenders collapse on you.

Use your finger pads. The ball should contact the finger pads with each bounce. Never dribble the ball with the palm of the hand. Keeping the ball on your finger pads will provide more control and make it less likely that you will commit a dribbling violation, which would result in a turnover.

Keep the dribble low. Dribble the ball at about waist level to maintain control and minimize the chance that a defender can reach in and steal it between bounces. Protect the ball with the nondribbling arm and hand against a defender who is playing tight, aggressive defense and trying to steal it. Stay alert as to where your teammates are positioned in case you have to make a quick pass to get out of a jam.

Push the ball forward. When dribbling up the court at full speed, push the ball out in front of you to match the forward progress of your body. Don't let the ball get away from you as you run up the court—keep the dribble in control.

Isiah Thomas used his speed, quickness, and a variety of dribbling moves to effectively control the basketball, break down defenders, and attack the opponent's basket. Some of the dribbling moves he and other skilled dribblers commonly use include the crossover dribble, between-the-legs dribble, jab-step dribble, behind-the-back dribble, and stop-n-go dribble.

Other Dribbling Options   The crossover dribble (figure 5.2) requires a quick transfer of the ball between the hands to keep the defender off balance. To perform a crossover dribble, begin dribbling the basketball low on one side of your body using either the left or right hand. Quickly move the ball to the other side of your body by pushing it in front of your knees, crossing it over to the other side. This transfer of dribbling hands promotes a quick change of direction for the ball handler. As the ball reaches the other hand, continue dribbling up the court in a new direction.

Crossover Dribble

5.2   a. Dribble low to one side.   b. Transfer the ball.

The between-the-legs dribble (figure 5.3) requires a quick scissors type of dribble to transfer the basketball from one hand to the other. To perform a between-the-legs dribble, begin dribbling the ball up the court with the right hand on the right side of the body. Take a step forward with the left foot—this creates a gap between the legs for the ball to pass through. Quickly push the basketball through the gap between your legs with the right hand, transferring the ball to the left hand. The ball should travel in a front-to-back or side-to-side direction when transferring hands. As the ball reaches the left hand, continue dribbling up the court in a new direction.

5.3 **Between the legs.**

The jab-step dribble (figure 5.4) requires the use of an effective jab step to cause the defender to move. To perform a jab-step dribble, begin dribbling the basketball up the court with the right hand. Focus on a spot on the floor where a defender is set on defense. Right before you reach the designated spot on the floor where the defender is set on defense, take a quick jab step to the left with the left foot to cause the defender to move to your left. Follow the jab step by pushing off the left foot to move back to the right. This pushoff from the left foot should move you in the opposite direction the defender is moving. Continue dribbling to the right at full speed.

Jab-Step Dribble

5.4   **a. Jab step to one side.**   **b. Quickly move to the other side.**

Behind-the-Back Dribble   The behind-the-back dribble (figure 5.5) requires the use of mechanics similar to the behind-the-back pass. It is an effective move used to change dribbling direction without having to transfer the ball in front of the body, minimizing the risk of a defender stealing the ball. To attempt a behind-the-back dribble, begin dribbling up the court with the left hand. As the ball bounces up into your left hand, use your left hand and arm to quickly swing the ball around your back to the right side of your body. Immediately find the basketball with your right hand and continue dribbling the ball up the court in the new direction.

Behind the Back

| 5.5 | a. Dribble up court. | b. Swing the ball behind your back to your other hand. |

Stop-n-Go Dribble The stop-n-go dribble uses a change in dribbling speeds to keep a defender off balance. To perform the stop-n-go dribble, begin dribbling up the court using the right hand. Quickly stop forward motion, dribbling once or twice while stationary for one second, and then continue dribbling up the court, possibly changing directions through the use of a previously described dribbling move (crossover, behind-the-back, between-the-legs, etc.). Randomly use this unpredictable stop-n-go movement as you advance the ball up the court toward the opponent's basket.

Ball Handling Without a Dribble   For many basketball players, the initial step toward developing dribbling skills is to establish basic ball-handling skills first. Ball-handling skills can help a player develop better control and feel for the basketball, and also assist with the development of enhanced hand-eye coordination. Ball-handling skills can be developed anywhere by anyone: Only a basketball and desire are necessary. Here are some practice activities that can help develop ball-handling skills but don't require a dribble.

5.6   a. Fingertip control.

■ Fingertip control (figure 5.6a). Extend your arms vertically over your head while holding a basketball. Quickly transfer the ball back and forth between the hands, allowing the ball to touch only your fingertips. Do at least 20 repetitions to warm up your hands.

■ Ball smacks (figure 5.6b). While holding a basketball in front of you, slap or spank the ball as hard as you can as you transfer the ball from hand to hand. Your hands should create a loud smacking sound on the ball. Do at least 20 repetitions to warm up your hands.

5.6 **b. Ball smacks.**

5.6 **c. Circles.**

■ Circles (figure 5.6c). Using both hands, transfer a basketball around different sections of your body in a circular motion. Start by doing circles around your head, then around your waist, and finally around your knees. Do at least 20 repetitions to warm up your hands.

■ Figure eights (figure 5.6d). Position your feet shoulder-width apart in a parallel, stationary position. Use your hands to pass the ball between and around your legs in a figure-eight motion without letting the ball touch the ground. Do at least 20 repetitions to warm up your hands.

5.6 **d. Figure eights.**

Dribbling With a Purpose

Properly executed dribbling skills can enhance a team's offensive potential in numerous ways in game situations. Good dribbling can improve a potential passing angle to a teammate, create an open perimeter shot, initiate a dribble-drive to the basket, protect a team's possession of the basketball during close games, or help in initiating and controlling a fast break.

The crossover dribble is effective when a player needs to change direction quickly. It is commonly used when an offensive player is trying to create an open shot, or when dribbling the ball up the court against tight defensive pressure.

The between-the-legs dribble is effective when a player needs to quickly change directions but doesn't want to dribble the ball out in front of the defender. It is commonly used when dribbling the ball up the court against tight defensive pressure, or when changing directions to initiate a dribble-drive to the basket.

The jab-step dribble is effective when a player needs to fake or shake a defender without changing dribbling directions. It is commonly used on a dribble-drive to the basket or in a fast-break situation.

The behind-the-back dribble is effective when a player needs to quickly change dribbling hands when moving at full speed up the court. It is commonly used in transitions and fast-break situations.

The stop-n-go dribble is effective against a defender playing tight, aggressive defense. It is commonly used when dribbling against a full-court, pressure, man-to-man defense.

Give it a go: Dribbling

BALL-HANDLING DRILLS WITH NO DRIBBLE

Practice common ball-handling drills without a dribble, such as fingertip control, ball smacks, circles, and figure eights. Complete at least 20 repetitions of each drill without losing control of the basketball before moving to the next one.

RIGHT-HANDED AND LEFT-HANDED DRIBBLING

In a stationary position, incorporate the basic fundamentals of dribbling as you complete 25 dribbling repetitions with each hand.

To practice scissors or figure-eight dribbling, dribble between your legs with each bounce as you slowly advance the ball up the court. Use your hands to pass the ball between your legs in a scissors or figure-eight motion. Gradually increase the speed of the drill as you get more proficient at dribbling between your legs.

To practice full-court dribbling using a variety of dribbling moves, dribble the length of the court as you practice each of the fundamental dribbling moves introduced in this chapter: right-hand speed dribble, left-hand speed dribble, jab-step dribble, crossover dribble, behind-the-back dribble, between-the-legs dribble, and stop-n-go dribble. Attempt the selected dribbling move at each quarter-court line (free-throw lines and half-court line).

TEN-SECOND DRILL

Start at the baseline. A defender tries to create a 10-second viola-tion by not allowing you to dribble past the half-court line within 10 seconds. You can use any type of dribbling move to avoid the 10-second violation. If you don't get the ball past the half-court line within 10 seconds, you have to complete five jumping jacks, knee-highs, or other basic conditioning activity. If the defender allows you past the half-court line within 10 seconds, he or she has to complete the conditioning activity. Switch from offense to defense after each practice trial.

NUMBERS

Participants form four to five lines on one of the baselines. A coach at center court extends an arm high above his or her head and holds up a certain number of fingers. Players begin to dribble up the court, keeping their heads up so they can see the coach's hand. The players must call out the number of fingers the coach is holding up. Have the coach change the number of fingers being held up every second or two. This activity develops the habit of keeping the head up when dribbling so the player can see the entire court.

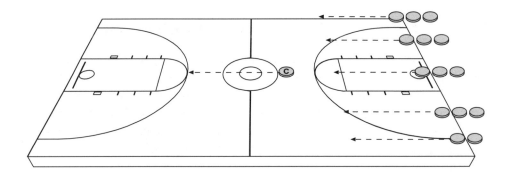

DRIBBLE TAG

Select two to three players to be taggers; everyone else is an avoider. Identify which area on the court players will be allowed to dribble in (full court, half court, inside the three-point line, etc.). Avoiders continuously dribble around the designated dribbling area as the tag-gers (who are also dribbling) try to tag them. If an avoider gets tagged or loses control of the basketball, he or she must quickly move out of the dribbling area and complete five jumping jacks, knee-highs, or other basic conditioning activity, and then reenter the game. A tagger who loses control of his or her basketball must also complete a quick conditioning activity before reentering the game. Change taggers at the end of each three- to five-minute round.

STATIONARY DRIBBLING

Attempt any ball-handling or dribbling drill described in the chapter, using the scoring guideline in table 5.1 to evaluate your performance.

TABLE 5.1 30-SECOND OR 60-SECOND TESTS

30-second test	60-second test
More than 20 = Hall-of-famer	More than 40 = Hall-of-famer
16 to 19 dribbles = MVP	34 to 39 dribbles = MVP
12 to 15 dribbles = All-star	25 to 33 dribbles = All-star
7 to 11 dribbles = Starter	15 to 25 dribbles = Starter
0 to 6 dribbles = Keep practicing	0 to 8 dribbles = Keep practicing

TECHNIQUE CHECKLISTS

Instructors and players can use technique checklists to check for specific fundamentals of dribbling technique or dribbling moves.

Dribbling Technique Checklist

_____ Dribble with head up

_____ Waist-high dribble

_____ Ball contacting the finger pads

_____ Dribble well with either hand

_____ Use nondribbling arm and hand to protect

Dribbling Moves Checklist

_____ Jab-step dribble

_____ Crossover dribble

_____ Between-the-legs dribble

_____ Stop-n-go dribble

_____ Behind-the-back dribble

_____ Change-of-pace dribble

6 CHAPTER

Screening

The screen is an essential ingredient of half-court offensive basketball. To be successful on offense, all five players on the court must have the ability to set fundamentally sound screens. Screens are frequently used in set offensive plays to create open shots for a team's best shooters. They are also commonly used in two-player offensive situations, such as the screen-and-roll. The effective use of screens will result in an offensive team being able to create high-percentage scoring chances.

Throughout his career, Karl Malone has effectively set screens in many different offensive situations. His wide, solid, muscular frame has proven to be the perfect obstacle to use for screening defenders trying to guard his teammates. Along with his sidekick John Stockton, Malone has perfected the use of the screen-and-roll, a popular two-player, half-court offensive set. By keeping himself in peak physical condition and by perfecting the screen-and-roll with John Stockton, Karl Malone has been able to amass more than 30,000 points and 10,000 rebounds during his exceptional NBA career.

Setting the Screen

The first step in setting a screen is to determine where and for whom you will set the screen. Once this is decided, you should move towards the teammate you want to set a screen for, or establish position on the court so that your teammate can move towards your screen. Prepare for contact with the defender you will set the screen on as you approach that player (or as that defender approaches you) (figure 6.1a). The contact, or collision, that occurs between the screener and defender is one of the most important elements of successful screens. Offensive teammates want this contact to occur so that the defender can get rubbed off into the screen. This action will hopefully provide a brief window of opportunity for the offensive player to receive the basketball for a shot, pass, or dribble-drive to the basket.

Just prior to setting the screen and contact with the defender, make sure your feet are stationary and you have established a wide, solid base with your feet (figure 6.1b). Protect yourself during the contact by positioning your hands low by your mid-section. Avoid leaning or moving into the defender during the contact. A moving screen is illegal and may result in an offensive foul called on you. Also avoid taking advantage of unsuspecting defenders who are run into screens they may not see, such as back screens. Promote sportsmanship by setting clean and effective screens without trying to hurt or injure your opponent.

Once your teammate uses the screen, and contact has been made with the defender, you should immediately try to do something productive on offense that will help your team score. If the screen you set was in the post area close to the basket, a quick pivot to open yourself up to the basketball may create an inside shot for you if the point can get you the ball quickly. If you set the screen on the perimeter, rolling to the basket looking for a pass from your teammate who used the screen (screen-and-roll) or moving to an open area of the court to position yourself for a perimeter shot are two simple ways to help your team generate a high-percentage shot.

6.1   a. Approach the defender from an angle.

6.1   b. Establish good screening position.

Responsibilities of the Cutter   The cutter's responsibilities are as important as the screener's responsibilities. First, the cutter must be patient, allowing the screener to set the screen. If the cutter is not patient and cuts before the screen is adequately set, the defender will see the screen being set, and will be able to avoid it. No offensive advantage will be gained.

Second, the cutter should always rub shoulders with the screener (figure 6.2) so that the defender will be rubbed off into the screen. If the cutter doesn't cut close enough to the screener to rub shoulders, the defender will be able to step around the screen easily.

Third, the use of a simple jab step by the cutter may enhance the effectiveness of a screen. To incorporate a jab step, the cutter should take the jab step in the opposite direction from where the screen is being set, then promptly move back toward the screen and rub shoulders with the screener. This action will increase the chance of the cutter running the defender into the screen.

Finally, the cutter must respond effectively to how the defender reacts to the screen. For example, if the defender tries to go behind a screen rather than step over or through it, the cutter may have an open jump shot available once he or she receives a crisp pass from a teammate. By properly responding to the defender's reaction to the screen, the cutter should be able to create a positive result.

The screening fundamentals introduced in this chapter can be used to set a variety of screens—including on-the-ball screens, off-the-ball screens, down screens, and back screens—at different spots on the court.

On-the-Ball Screens   An on-the-ball screen (figure 6.3) is a screen set for the offensive player who has possession of the ball (the point). Once the screen is set, the point can utilize the screen in different ways, depending on how the

6.2   **Rub shoulders.**

defense responds to the screen. If the defender can't fight through the screen or moves behind the screen, the point may have enough space to immediately shoot a jump shot or dribble-drive to the basket. If a defender does try to fight through a screen, the point may have a chance to dribble-drive directly to the basket.

In many cases, an on-the-ball screen can evolve into a screen-and-roll situation between the screener and the point, an offensive play made famous by John Stockton and Karl Malone. For the screen-and-roll, the screener sets a pick on the defender guarding the point. After the point uses the screen, the screener pivots or rolls open to where the ball is on the court, followed by a movement toward the basket. The screener holds up a target hand, hoping for a quick pass from the point for an easy lay-up.

Another option for the screener after an on-the-ball screen is to pop out to an open spot on the perimeter, looking for a pass from the point so that a jump shot can be taken.

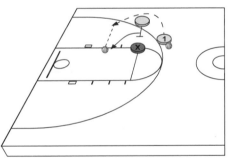

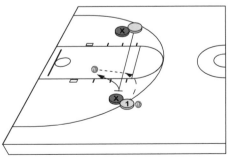

6.3   **On-the-ball screen.**

Off-the-Ball Screens   An off-the-ball screen (figure 6.4) is a screen set for an offensive player who doesn't have possession of the basketball. In many cases, an off-the-ball screen is set away from the position of the ball on the court. A cutter can use the screen to cut toward the ball or basket, where he or she should receive a pass from the point. Off-the-ball screens are used by both perimeter and post players to create cutting and ball-receiving opportunities for offensive teammates. The effective use of an off-the-ball screen often leads to a high-percentage shot close to the basket.

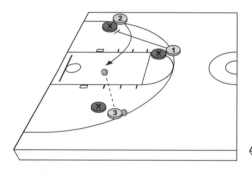
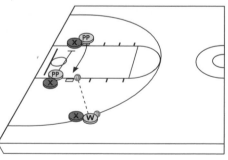

6.4   Off-the-ball screen.

Down Screens A down screen (figure 6.5) is usually set around the block area close to the three-second lane. It allows a player to cut away from the baseline to an open area of the court to receive the basketball. Down screens can be used to create scoring opportunities for both perimeter and post players. The screener typically starts from a free-throw line elbow position and moves down toward a teammate positioned on the block close to the basket. Once the screen is set, the cutter uses it to move from the baseline to an open area of the court where a pass can be received.

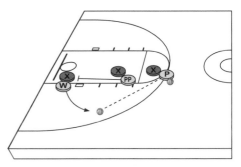

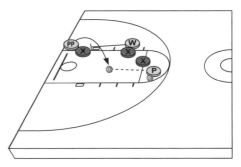

6.5 Down screen.

Back Screens A back screen (figure 6.6) can be set for both perimeter and post players at any spot on the court, although typically is set along the baseline and wing. Usually a back screen is set in a position so that the defender can't see the screener. However, the screener must leave enough room for the defender to take one step before any potential contact with the screener is made. Back screens can enhance the element of surprise on the defender and often lead to easy baskets for the offensive team.

6.6 Back screen.

Take it to the court

Setting the Right Screen

During a game, many offensive situations arise in which a screen is appropriate. Which screen to use depends on the specific game situation.

On-the-ball screens are effective in screen-and-roll situations between offensive teammates and when trying to create a dribble-drive opportunity for the point. An on-the-ball screen can also help create an opportunity for an open jump shot.

Down screens are useful for either a post or perimeter player situated in the block area. The down screen may help a post player shed the defender so that he or she can make a curl cut toward the basket. A down screen may also help a perimeter player make a cut from the baseline out to the wing area to receive a pass and take an open perimeter jump shot.

Back screens are good for post and wing players, especially if a defender is playing overly aggressive defense. The back screen can help create an opportunity for a backdoor cut to the basket, followed by an easy lay-up opportunity.

Mid-court screens can help free a point guard from defensive pressure, especially versus a pressing defense. Against zone defenses, screens by wing and post players can help create zone gaps between defenders and open spaces for players to take perimeter jump shots. The use of screens during inbounds plays helps free up offensive players to successfully receive the inbounds pass.

Give it a go: Screening

SCREENING PRACTICE

For individual practice, set up two chairs to be an offensive player and a defender. Practice setting screens on the defender using the recommended fundamentals.

If you have practice partners available, replace the chairs with your teammates. Practice setting screens on the defender using the recommended fundamentals. Players should switch positions after every two to three repetitions.

SCREEN-AND-ROLL

Divide class participants into groups of three: a point, a defender on the point, and a screener (figure 6.7). Starting at half-speed, the screener sets a screen on the defender, then rolls to the basket looking for a pass from the point. The point delivers a pass to the screener, who shoots a lay-up or other appropriate shot. The screener also practices popping out to the perimeter for a pass or a jump shot after the point utilizes the screen. Practice the screen-and-roll at various spots on the court. Players should switch positions after every two to three practice trials. The defender should gradually increase defensive intensity. Add a second defender on the screener to allow the drill to evolve into a 2-on-2 game.

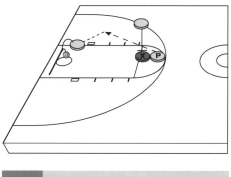

6.7 Setup for the screen-and-roll drill.

DOWN-SCREEN DRILL

This drill requires five participants (figure 6.8). The point stands on the perimeter. One offensive player and one defensive player stand at the elbow of the free-throw line. The other offensive player and defensive player stand in the post area (block). The offensive player at the free-throw line practices setting down screens for the offensive player in the post. The point passes the ball to the post offensive player as he or she cuts to an open area of the court. Rotate positions after every two to three practice trials. A defender may be added on the point to allow the drill to evolve into a 3-on-3 game.

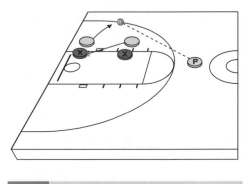

6.8 Setup for the down screen drill.

SCREEN AWAY/CUT TOWARD

In a half-court, 5-on-5 situation, teams scrimmage against each other with emphasis placed on screening away from the basketball and cutting toward the basketball into open areas of the court. No dribbling is allowed. A minimum of three passes must precede a shot. Shots must be taken within the three-second lane. If a shot is taken outside the three-second lane or before three passes have been made, the game is temporarily paused and all offensive players must complete five jumping jacks, knee-highs, or other conditioning activity. All defensive players complete a similar conditioning activity if the offense is allowed to score an uncontested lay-up.

TECHNIQUE CHECKLISTS

Instructors and players can use technique checklists to check for skill development on screening technique or specific screening-cutting options.

Screening Technique Checklist

_____ Appropriate angle for screen
_____ Solid stance and base
_____ Feet shoulder-width apart
_____ Hands protecting midsection
_____ No leaning or moving into offensive player

Screening/Cutting Options

_____ On-the-ball screen
_____ Screen-and-roll
_____ Off-the-ball screen
_____ Jab Step before cutting
_____ Screen away/cut toward
_____ Down screen
_____ Back screen for wing or post

Individual Defense

Individual defense is the key to overall team defense. A basketball team's defense can only be as strong as the team's weakest individual defender. Therefore, all players on the court must be fundamentally sound on defense. Great individual defenders are able to minimize an offensive player's number of touches of the ball, which decreases the number of scoring opportunities that offensive player has during a game. Attributes of great individual defenders include aggressiveness, determination, confidence, quickness, body-balance, effective use of the hands and arms, vision, communication, hustle, and personal fitness. Great defenders use heart, head, and feet to create positive results while maintaining individual defensive intensity throughout the game.

Gary Payton excels at individual defensive fundamentals and has established himself as one of the premier defensive players in the NBA. Gary averages over two steals per game and usually succeeds at shutting down the opponent's best offensive player, thus earning himself the nickname "The Glove." His defensive abilities have not gone unnoticed. He has been selected to the NBA's All-Defensive First Team for eight consecutive seasons (1994 through 2001).

Getting Defensive

The importance of defense in the game of basketball cannot be underestimated. Every basketball player will spend approximately 50 percent of each game playing defense and protecting the basket. The individual or team that is more effective on defense usually wins the game. Therefore it is important to spend a comparable percentage of practice time (approximately 50 percent) developing individual defensive skills and talents. Individual defensive skills and habits developed during practice will transfer smoothly over to game-play and will ultimately increase a team's chances of winning basketball games.

The first step in developing individual defensive skills is to become familiar and comfortable with the fundamental defensive stance. The fundamental defensive stance can be considered a basic ready position. It places a defender in an athletic stance that promotes quick, balanced movement in any direction, allowing a defender to stay with or shadow the offensive player he is guarding. Quick movement in this defensive stance will help a defender stick with an offensive player like glue wherever he or she moves on the court, which may frustrate the opponent.

To assume this basic individual defensive stance (figure 7.1a), stand with your feet shoulder-width apart in a slightly staggered stance. Your weight should be on the balls of your feet. Knees are

7.1 **a. Defensive stance.**

flexed. Bend forward slightly at the waist, keeping your back straight. Extend your arms into potential passing lanes (figure 7.1b). Follow the basketball with your hands and fingers, ready to intercept a pass or block a shot. Keep your head lower than the offensive player's head (about chin level) while focusing your eyes on the waist or hips of the offensive player, rather than on the basketball. This will minimize the effectiveness of the offensive player's ball fake.

Use this individual defensive stance any time the offensive player you are guarding is able to assume possession of the basketball. Consistently use the "one arm's length" rule when establishing the distance that needs to be maintained between you and the offensive player. The rationale for implementing this rule is simple. Positioning yourself too close to the offensive player (less than one arm's length) may allow the offensive player to easily dribble-drive past you to the basket. Positioning yourself too far away from the offensive player (more than one arm's length) may allow the offensive player to shoot uncontested jump shots over you. Maintaining the one arm's length distance hopefully will limit offensive options for your opponent and force your opponent to pass the ball to a teammate positioned away from your basket.

7.1   **b. Extend your arms into the passing lanes.**

Moving Laterally: Slide-Steps Quick slide-steps will help a defender move laterally quickly. With slide-steps, a defender's feet skim or slide across the surface of the court in the direction the defender wants to travel. For example, if the offensive player you are guarding dribbles to your right, push off the ground using your left foot and leg to initiate movement to the right (figure 7.2a). Follow with a series of quick slide-steps. As your feet slide, or skim, across the court's surface, avoid letting your feet get too close together so that they do not get tangled (figure 7.2b). In fact, the heels of your feet should never touch each other during slide-steps. Stay low and maintain a balanced stance as you move. Extend your arms to minimize potential passing lanes for the offensive player.

Slide-Stepping

7.2   a. Push off the ground.

7.2   b. Feet skim across the floor.

Changing Directions: Drop-Steps If a defender needs to quickly change directions to keep pace with an offensive player who is dribbling the basketball, the defender should use a drop-step (figure 7.3). To perform a drop-step, begin by slowly slide-stepping to the right. After slide-stepping to the right, plant the right foot to stop the movement, then drop the left foot back or to the side in the new direction you want to move. Push off the ground using the right foot to initiate movement of the body to the left. Now begin slide-stepping to the left. Using drop-steps with slide-steps will cause the defender to travel in a zigzag path across the court as he or she tries to maintain a position between the offensive player and the basket.

Drop-Stepping

7.3   **a. Slide-step laterally.**

7.3   **b. Stop and drop to change direction.**

Defending a Post Player   Learning to effectively defend a post player is essential because an offensive priority for any team is to try to pass the basketball to a post player to create high-percentage shots close to the basket. Getting the ball to a post player is a great way for the offense to break down a half-court defense. When defending a post player, the defender has two basic options: Defend in front of the post player (between the post player and the ball) or defend behind the post player (between the post player and the basket). Either option can be effective as long as other team defenders are willing to provide help whenever necessary.

Playing behind the post player is usually discouraged because it allows the post player to easily receive the ball. This often provides the post player with potential high-percentage shots close to the basket or passing options to teammates spotting up for perimeter jump shots if their defender double-teams the post. Therefore, it is recommended that you deny the pass into the post by fronting the post player (figure 7.4).

To front a post player, position your shoulder and arm in the passing lane between the basketball and the post player. As the ball moves around the perimeter, make quick defensive position adjustments to maintain a fronting position by the post player. If the ball is lobbed over your head to the post player, your teammates positioned on the other side of the post player, if alert, will move over to provide help-side defense.

7.4   **Fronting the post player.**

Denying the Ball and Denying the Cut   A top priority of an individual defender playing man-to-man defense is to not allow the offensive player he or she is guarding to receive the basketball. If the offensive player cannot receive the basketball, he or she cannot score. This is usually referred to as denying the ball or denying the pass (figure 7.5a). The keys for denying the ball are to move quickly on defense in order to stay within one arm's length of the offensive player you are guarding, and always have an arm and hand in the passing lane between the offensive player and the basketball.

Another important individual defensive fundamental is referred to as denying the cut (figure 7.5b). If an offensive player you are guarding does not have the basketball, he or she is going to work hard to receive it. He or she will probably try to cut to an open area of the court to receive a pass from a teammate. An individual defender must try to not allow the offensive player to make this cut. To deny the cut, you must first anticipate the cut, stepping into the path of the offensive player by using your body to obstruct the cutting lane. This will force the offensive player to move away from the basket, or open area of the court, to receive the ball.

7.5   a. Defensive goal 1: Deny the ball.

b. Defensive goal 2: Deny the cut.

If the offensive player does receive the basketball, the defensive goal immediately changes from denying the ball or cut to denying the dribble-drive or open shot (figure 7.5c). Denying the dribble-drive will make it difficult for the offensive player to dribble close to the basket for a high-percentage shot. If the defensive player can deny an open shot or dribble-drive, and force the offensive player to pass the basketball to a teammate, the defensive player has temporarily triumphed, and has won one of the many individual offense–defense player battles that will occur throughout a game.

7.5 **c. Defensive goal 3: Deny the dribble-drive to the basket.**

Take it to the court

Communicating on Defense

Communicating with teammates while playing individual defense is an important key to successful team defense during games. Individual defenders must talk to each other throughout the game to enhance overall team defense.

The phrases "screen right" or "screen left" help a defensive teammate know that a screen is being set and the side it is being set on. "Shot" helps defensive teammates know when a shot has been taken so that defenders can box out offensive players and establish position for a defensive rebound. "Switch" helps a defensive teammate know to switch offensive players to guard if a teammate has been screened. "You got ball, I got back" helps a defensive player identify his responsibility during a fast-break situation, either to stop the offensive player with the basketball or to assume a position in the three-second lane to defend the basket. "Cutter high," "cutter middle," or "cutter low" warns defenders when offensive players cut or move into certain areas of the three-second lane. "Cutter high" refers to the free-throw line area, "cutter middle" to the middle of the lane, and "cutter low" to the post/block area.

Give it a go: Individual Defense

QUICK FEET

A teacher or coach faces a player who has assumed the fundamental defensive position. At the start signal, the teacher or coach points in different directions and the player practices using slide-steps and drop-steps to move in the appropriate directions (figure 7.6).

7.6 **Quick-feet drill.**

FULL-COURT 1-ON-1 DRIBBLE

Divide players into partners, one offensive player and one defensive player. Position partners behind one of the baselines of the court. The defensive player moves onto the court and assumes the fundamental defensive stance. He or she will practice using slide-steps and drop-steps while playing defense against the offensive player. The offensive player dribbles the ball the length of the court. The goal for the defensive player is to cut off the offensive player's forward progress, forcing a change of dribbling direction. The players switch positions after each attempt.

CLASS DIRECTIONAL DRILL

Players spread out on the court and face the coach. At the sound of the whistle, the coach points in different directions while participants use quick, efficient slide-steps and drop-steps to move in the direction indicated by the coach (figure 7.7). Players who move in the wrong direction must quickly move to the sidelines and complete a short conditioning activity, such as 10 jumping jacks, knee-highs, or push-ups, before rejoining the drill.

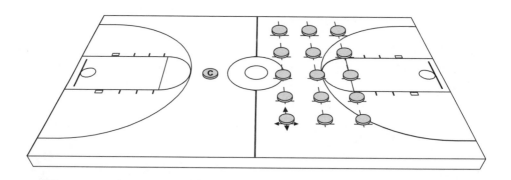

7.7 Class directional drill.

SELF-TEST/INDIVIDUAL SKILLS TEST

You can test yourself using one of the previous practice activities or other useful individual defensive practice activities. Create a scoring guideline like the one shown in table 7.1 to evaluate performance.

TABLE 7.1 INDIVIDUAL QUICK-FEET DRILL

Players use slide-steps to move back and forth from one side of the three-second lane to the other. They must touch the lane blocks as they move from side to side.

30-second test	60-second test
More than 30 lane slides = Hall-of-famer	More than 55 lane slides = Hall-of-famer
26 to 30 lane slides = MVP	48 to 54 lane slides = MVP
19 to 25 lane slides = All-star	40 to 47 lane slides = All-star
10 to 18 lane slides = Starter	30 to 39 lane slides = Starter
0 to 10 lane slides = Keep practicing	0 to 30 lane slides = Keep practicing

TECHNIQUE CHECKLISTS

Instructors and players can use technique checklists to check for skill development with the individual defensive stance or with specific individual defensive fundamentals, such as communication.

Individual Defensive Position Checklist

_____ Feet shoulder-width apart
_____ Slightly staggered stance
_____ Knees flexed
_____ Back straight
_____ Arms and fingers extended
_____ Eyes focused on offensive player's hips, not basketball

Defensive Communication Checklist

_____ Calling out screens
_____ Calling out side of body for screens (right or left)
_____ Calling out defensive switches
_____ Calling out shots taken
_____ Calling out fast-break responsibility
_____ Calling out cutters

Rebounding

If a basketball team wants to reduce the number of scoring opportunities for its opponent and produce more second-chance scoring opportunities for its own team, all five players on the court must be committed to rebounding. Rebounding will help a team control the boards and win the battle of ball possession during each game. Rebounding is a skill every player can develop. All it takes is a little determination, good positioning, and timing. Defensive rebounding can reduce the number of shots for an opponent, whereas offensive rebounding can produce high-percentage, second-chance shots for your team. In many cases, the team that accumulates the most rebounds during a game will earn the victory.

Does a player have to be tall and have great jumping ability to be a good rebounder? Although height and jumping ability can prove helpful for rebounders, the effective use of rebounding fundamentals is the key to rebounding success. In the past 25 years, no player has been a more effective rebounder than Dennis Rodman. Rodman's playing height was listed at 6 feet, 8 inches, four to six inches shorter than the typical center in the NBA. However, the "Worm" relentlessly crashed the boards during his career, winning seven consecutive rebounding titles during the 1990s. Determination and good positioning led Dennis to an average of 13 rebounds per game throughout his career.

Boxing Out

As with each skill in the game of basketball, rebounding requires the effective use of basic fundamentals to maximize your success. Boxing out your opponent puts you in a good position to secure the rebound and may prevent your opponent from getting it.

Establishing a good rebounding position is the first step to becoming an effective rebounder. As soon as you know, see, or hear that a shot has been taken, quickly move toward the player you are guarding and make body contact (figure 8.1a). Use a hand or arm to keep track of your opponent's position on the court. Follow the body contact with a quick pivot so that you can see the basket (figure 8.1b). Drive your backside into the opponent's midsection to limit his or her lateral movement. Bend your knees to lower your center of gravity and to establish a firm, leveraged position so that your opponent cannot move you. You have now boxed out your opponent and have established good rebounding positioning on the court.

Initially, use your arms and hands to help feel or identify your opponent's position on the court, but do not hold or grab your opponent when trying to establish a box-out position—this will result in a defensive foul on you. Once you have identified your opponent's location and have established sound position with your lower body,

8.1 **a. Make contact with the player you are guarding.** **b. Pivot and get in low body position.**

extend your arms and hands to shoulder level and point your elbows out (figure 8.1c). As the ball bounces off the rim, extend your arms toward the ball and aggressively elevate off the ground (figure 8.1d). Grab the rebound using both hands to secure possession of the ball.

If an offensive player tries to reach in for the ball, use your body to protect the ball by establishing a pivot foot and pivoting to move your body between the defender and the basketball.

Great rebounders not only establish fundamentally sound box-out position on the court; they also develop a keen sense of timing when jumping for a rebound. When timing your jump, try to predict how high and how far the ball will bounce off the rim and in which direction. The ball often bounces to the opposite side of the basket from where the original shot was taken. Rebounding practice will help you develop timing so that you will elevate for a rebound at the most opportune moment.

c. Reach toward the basket.

d. Elevate for the rebound.

Passing the Ball to the Outlet Man   Once you have secured a rebound, it is essential that you accurately pass the ball to an "outlet," or ball possession may be lost. An outlet is a teammate who is quick and possesses excellent dribbling and passing skills, such as the point guard. A teammate designated as the outlet must clearly communicate his or her court position to you so that you can pass the ball to him or her. A quick pass to the outlet (figure 8.2) can produce fast-break scoring chances if the opponent is slow in transitioning from offense to defense. Once the outlet receives the pass, he or she should dribble the ball to the middle of the court and attack the opponent's basket as quickly as possible.

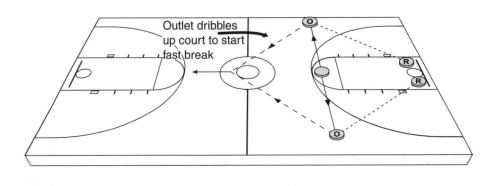

Outlet dribbles up court to start fast break

8.2   **Outlet positions.**

Court Position   Skilled rebounders are able to establish box-ing-out position in appropriate areas on the court. For example, a defensive player who establishes rebounding position too close to or underneath the basket will have a minimal chance of getting the rebound because the ball will probably bounce over his or her head, away from the basket. Players should establish rebounding position a few feet from the basket, but never underneath it, to compensate for the bounce (figure 8.3).

Offensive Rebounding   Offensive rebounding is an important basketball fundamental because it can help the offensive team produce high-percentage, second-chance shots. Offensive rebounding is probably more difficult than defensive rebounding because the defender is usually positioned between the basket and the offensive player when a shot is taken. Once a shot is taken, offensive players must move quickly to get around the defensive players in order to establish advantageous rebounding position by the basket. They must try to achieve this without causing too much contact with the defensive player or they may get called for an unnecessary offensive foul.

The spin move (figure 8.4) can help an offensive player avoid getting fully boxed out by a defensive player. When a shot is taken and the defensive player tries to establish box-out position, plant either foot on the court to establish a pivot foot and then quickly pivot in a direction that will open you up to the basket as the ball bounces off the rim. Hold your hands high to anticipate the ball's path. Using the spin move will help you establish at least a side rebounding position rather than being fully boxed out by the defender.

8.3 **Good rebounding position.**

Spin Move

8.4 **a. Plant your pivot foot.**   **b. Pivot to the basket, arms extended.**

The fake-n-step move (figure 8.5) helps an offensive player avoid being totally boxed out by a defender and leads to good offensive rebounding position. This move is sometimes used in free throw situations. To perform a fake-n-step, take a step or two in one direction as a defender tries to set box-out position on you. Right before the defender sets lower body position on you, move quickly in the other direction and use a high, strong forward step to position at least one leg in front of the defender. This strong step will put you in rebounding position to the side or in front of the defensive player.

Fake-n-Step

8.5 **a. Step in one direction, getting the defender to move with you.**

8.5 **b. Fake out the defender by strongly stepping in the other direction.**

In some rebounding situations, an offensive player may not be able to grab a rebound with both hands to secure it but may be able to extend one arm up to the basket as the ball bounces off the rim and tip the ball back into the basket. This is called a tip-in (figure 8.6) and requires a perfectly timed jump and arm extension. When attempting an offensive tip, make sure the ball is out of the basket cylinder. Otherwise, you may be called for offensive goaltending, meaning the basket will not count.

8.6 The tip-in.

In Pursuit of the Rebound

During a typical basketball game, most teams make fewer than 50 percent of the shots they attempt. Keeping this statistic in mind, the team that does a better job of rebounding missed shots to gain possession (defensive rebounding) or maintain possession (offensive rebounding) of the ball will have an advantage. It makes sense that the team that accumulates the most total rebounds (defensive and offensive) usually wins the game.

During a game, all five defensive players on the court have the responsibility to box out the offensive players they are guarding and pursue the rebound when the offense attempts a shot. Once a shot is taken, all five defenders must try to establish good rebounding position between the basket and the offensive players they are guarding. This is followed by aggressively going after the ball as it bounces off the rim.

Offensive players must also pursue the rebound once a teammate takes a shot. They must assume that the shot will miss and try to position themselves in good rebounding position between the basket and the defenders who are guarding them. Even if good rebounding position cannot be gained, offensive players should at least try to elevate to the basket to tip the ball in for a score as the ball comes off the rim. However, an offensive player must be careful not to cause too much contact with a defensive player when elevating for a potential tip-in basket. This may result in an unnecessary offensive foul (such as an over-the-back foul). In addition, at least one offensive player (usually the point) should stay back toward center court to protect against a fast break by the opponent.

Free-throw situations are key moments during a game in which rebounding fundamentals must be used by defensive players in order to secure possession of the basketball. Following a free-throw attempt, defensive players must seal off offensive players with a sound box-out so that if the free throw misses, the defense will have a better chance of getting the rebound, minimizing second-chance shots by the offense.

Give it a go: Rebounding

OFFENSIVE TIP DRILL

Using one hand, try to tip the ball off a wall or the backboard 10 consecutive times (figure 8.7). Elevate off the ground before each ball contact. Try to tip the ball into the basket on the 10th tip. Once you reach 10 consecutive tips, increase your goal to 20.

To turn this into a group drill, divide into groups of 7 to 10 players. Each group is assigned to a basket and forms a single-file line on either side of the basket. Using one basketball, each player tries to tip the ball off the backboard as the next teammate follows immediately after, keeping the ball from bouncing on the ground for as long as possible. Each player must elevate off the ground when tipping the ball. The last player tries to tip the ball into the basket for a score. Have a friendly competition to see which group can produce the most consecutive tips.

8.7 Individual offensive tip drill.

BOX-OUT DRILL

Divide into groups of three players (shooter, offensive player, and defensive player; figure 8.8). Have the shooter take shots from a variety of spots on the court. The defensive player should use rebounding fundamentals to box out the offensive player and secure the rebound. The offensive player should use an offensive move (spin or fake-n-step) to try to get the rebound. If the offensive player secures the rebound, the defensive player must complete five knee-highs, push-ups, jumping jacks, or other type of conditioning activity. If the defensive player secures the rebound three consecutive times, the offensive player must complete a similar conditioning activity. Rotate positions after every three to five shots.

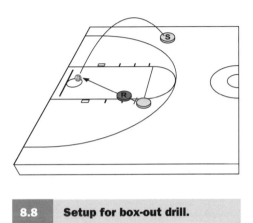

8.8 Setup for box-out drill.

3-ON-3, 4-ON-4, 5-ON-5 REBOUNDING

Divide into groups of three, four, or five, and assign two groups to each basket. One group will play offense and the other will play defense. The offense moves the ball quickly around the court. No more than five passes can be made before a shot is taken. When a shot is taken, all defenders use rebounding fundamentals to box out the offensive players they are guarding. If one of the offensive players gets the rebound, the defenders must complete five knee-highs, push-ups, jumping jacks, or some other quick conditioning activity. If the defensive team secures the rebound three consecutive times, the offensive team completes a similar conditioning activity. Teams alternate from defense to offense after three to five practice trials. Rotate teams to different baskets every five minutes.

INDIVIDUAL SKILLS TEST/SELF-TEST

Use one of the rebounding drills in this chapter, such as the individual tip drill, as a self-test. Use a scoring guideline based on table 8.1.

TABLE 8.1 INDIVIDUAL OFFENSIVE TIP DRILL SELF-TEST SCORING

More than 15 consecutive tips	Hall-of-famer
11 to 15 consecutive tips	MVP
8 to 10 consecutive tips	All-star
5 to 7 consecutive tips	Starter
0 to 4 consecutive tips	Keep practicing

TECHNIQUE CHECKLIST

Instructors and players can use this technique checklist to check for skill development on defensive rebounding fundamentals.

Rebounding Technique Checklist

_____ Establishes a wide, solid base

_____ Flexes knees for body leverage

_____ Demonstrates good high positioning of arms, elbows, and hands

_____ Accurately times the jump

_____ Successfully gains possession of the basketball

_____ Makes an accurate pass to the outlet

Full-Court Offense

Full-court offense, otherwise known as the fast break, is one of the most exciting elements of basketball. When executed correctly, a fast break often results in a variety of lay-ups and high-percentage shots. For a team to effectively run a full-court offense, players must be fundamentally sound in many fast-paced basketball fundamentals. Players must also develop a fast-break mentality, always looking for the opportunity to create a quick score. Maintaining a high level of conditioning will help a team to be successful at full-court offense throughout a basketball game.

Over the past 25 years, the team that has probably best exemplified successful full-court offense is the Los Angeles Lakers of the 1980s. Led by Earvin "Magic" Johnson, the Lakers pushed the basketball up the court at every opportunity. With Magic at the point and James Worthy, Michael Cooper, and Byron Scott on the wings, the Lakers often put on a fast-break clinic during their games. The Lakers became so proficient at full-court offense that their games became known as "Showtime." Indeed, Magic and his L.A. crew put on a fast-break show, executing full-court offense to perfection to win five NBA championships during the 1980s.

The Fast Break

The main objective of full-court offense is to create quick and easy baskets before an opponent can adequately set up a defense. A team can become proficient at full-court offense if each player focuses on fast-break fundamentals: Gain possession of the basketball, pass the ball up the court, attack the opponent's basket, fill the lanes, and follow the shot.

9.1   a. Gain possession.

Gaining possession of the basketball (figure 9.1a) is achieved by getting a defensive rebound, stealing the ball, blocking a shot, or creating a turnover by the offense. This may also include gaining possession after an opponent's made basket.

Once the ball is in your possession, it should be quickly passed up the court (figure 9.1b). In general, passing the ball is recommended with fast-break basketball because a team can advance the ball up the

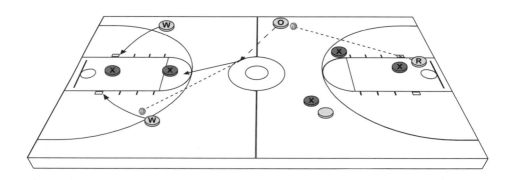

9.1   b. Pass the ball quickly up the court.

court more quickly by passing than dribbling, making it more likely that you can get a quick score. As the basketball is advanced up the court, the offensive team should attack the opponent's basket as soon as possible (figure 9.1c), before the opponent can get back on defense to protect its basket.

As offensive players approach the opponent's basket, they must stay spread out in individual lanes on the court. This will make a fast break more difficult to defend, improve passing lanes to teammates, and won't allow one defender to defend multiple offensive players at the same time.

9.1 **c. Attack the basket.**

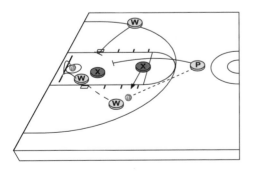

9.1 **d. Get in position to rebound.**

The offensive players who don't take the initial shot on the fast break should immediately position themselves close to the basket for the potential offensive rebound and a second-chance shot (figure 9.1d). If there is a numbers advantage on the fast break (e.g., 2-on-1 or 3-on-2), there will be too many offensive players for the defense to successfully box out.

The most common fast-break situations are the 2-on-1 and 3-on-2 fast breaks. Each situation demands different responsibilities from the offensive players involved. However, if each offensive player performs his or her job and employs fast-break fundamentals, the offense should be able to produce an easy basket.

2-on-1 Fast Break   A 2-on-1 fast break (figure 9.2) is probably the most advantageous fast break for an offensive team. In a 2-on-1 situation, there are twice as many offensive players as defensive players. This makes it very difficult for the sole defensive player to stop the offense from scoring an easy basket, usually a lay-up. The offensive players on the 2-on-1 fast break should stay spread out on the court while advancing toward the opponent's basket. This will help establish an excellent passing lane between the players and will require the defender to commit to guarding one of the offensive players, almost always the one who has possession of the basketball.

The ball handler should read the defender as he or she moves up the court. As the defender makes a defensive decision and commits to stopping the basketball, the offensive player should be able to identify the decision and respond accordingly. The response will be either a quick, precise pass to the second offensive player, or, if the defender hesitates in stopping the point, a dribble-drive directly to the basket for the lay-up. Either response should result in an easy basket for the offense.

Once up the court, the offensive players should attack the basket immediately. With only one defender guarding the basket, the offensive players can and should advance the ball aggressively to the basket. They should never settle for anything less than a lay-up during a 2-on-1 fast break. The worst-case scenario is that the defender will foul the shooter, resulting in two free-throw attempts for the offensive player.

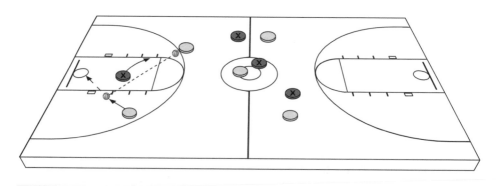

9.2   2-on-1 fast break.

Both offensive players must follow the initial shot by crashing the boards. If the first shot is missed, the chances are good that an offensive rebound can be secured and a second-chance shot taken because there will be only one defender trying to box out two offensive players.

3-on-2 Fast Break   A 3-on-2 fast break (figure 9.3) is also an advantageous situation for an offensive team. With proper court spacing, good decision making, precise passing, and aggressive movement toward the basket, an offensive team should be able to produce easy baskets from a 3-on-2 fast break.

The offensive players should stay spread out on the court. Being properly spaced will establish excellent passing lanes between the offensive players and create wide dribbling lanes to the basket between the two defenders.

After the offensive players cross the half-court line, the point should pass the ball to one of the wing players immediately. This should cause the back defender to move over to guard the wing who received the pass. This movement by the back defender should create a gap between the two defenders, possibly producing dribble-drive lanes to the basket. If the back defender is slow to cover the pass to the wing, the wing should aggressively advance the ball to the basket for a shot.

Once the point passes to the wing, he or she should establish a position around the free-throw line. This will promote good spacing between the three offensive players and, if necessary, place the point in a good position to receive a quick return pass from the wing. If a return pass is received, the point can either quickly reverse the ball to the other wing or dribble-drive straight to the basket if a lane has opened.

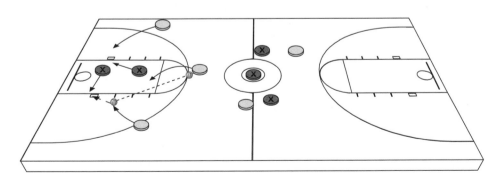

9.3   **3-on-2 fast break.**

The offensive player with the ball must attack the basket as soon as possible. Attacking the basket with a dribble-drive should result in a high-percentage shot, such as a lay-up. The worst-case scenario is that a defender will foul the shooter, resulting in two free-throw attempts for the offense.

Primary Fast Break Versus Secondary Fast Break The primary objective of full-court offense is to advance the basketball up the court as quickly as possible in order to create a player advantage against the opponent, such as 2-on-1 or 3-on-2. This is referred to as the primary fast break, and it usually does not include the use of structured offensive plays or sets. To be successful at the primary fast break, players need to develop specific basketball skills that are used in full-court offensive situations, such as full-speed dribbling, full-court passing, full-speed lay-ups, and passing to moving teammates.

If a team is unable to create an immediate numbers advantage against an opponent on the fast break, initial high-percentage scoring options from the primary fast break will probably not be available. However, as the remaining offensive players advance up the court, set cuts, movement patterns, and plays may be used to help the offense transition from the fast break into a regular half-court offense. This is referred to as the secondary fast break. The use of trailers (usually post players) and swing passes to perimeter players (usually wing players) for open jump shots are common offensive objectives of the secondary fast break.

Using the Outlet An important step for a team that has gained possession of the basketball and wants to create a fast-break opportunity is to advance the basketball up the court as quickly as possible. Though passing the ball up the court is faster than dribbling, in many situations a team will not be able to pass the ball directly up the court. In these situations, an outlet (figure 9.4) should be used.

The point guard is probably the best player to serve as the outlet because of his or her superior ball-handling, passing, and playmaking abilities. Post players, who typically rebound well, must deliver a pass to the outlet as soon as they secure the rebound or after a made shot.

The outlet must establish a position on the same side of the court as the rebounder. As soon as the outlet receives the basketball, it should be advanced to the middle of the court and toward the opponent's basket as wing players fill the court lanes on either side.

Using Trailers Post players, who usually secure defensive rebounds to initiate a primary fast break, often finish fast-break scoring

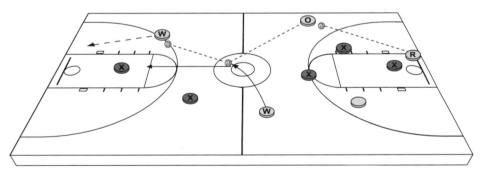

9.4   **Outlet.**

opportunities as trailers (figure 9.5). Post players are often overlooked by the defense because they follow the initial fast-break surge by the offense. A post player who aggressively advances up the court after making the initial pass to the outlet can make a cut to the basket to receive a pass for a high-percentage shot. Point guards and wings must keep trailers in sight as they make their way up the court to help finish the fast-break opportunity.

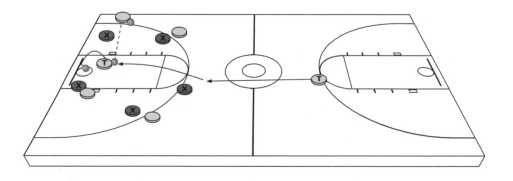

9.5 **Position of trailers.**

Developing a Fast-Break Mentality

Every basketball player must develop a fast-break mentality for a team to be successful at full-court offense. In simple terms, a fast-break mentality is continually focusing on trying to create fast-break opportunities whenever your team gains possession of the ball.

To develop a fast-break mentality, beginning basketball players should start by practicing the individual skills that represent parts of the overall fast-break opportunity. Practicing individual skills such as full-court dribbling, passing to moving teammates, full-court lay-ups, and passing to the outlet man will help beginning basketball players develop the basic skills necessary to successfully perform in a fast-break situation.

As players develop these individual skills and begin to participate in fast-break situations during basketball games, their confidence in their full-court offensive skills will grow and develop. As their confidence level and playing experience increase, players should start focusing on trying to create a fast-break situation every time their team gains possession of the ball.

Basketball coaches and teachers can also help players develop a fast-break mentality by consistently practicing and emphasizing fast-break fundamentals during basketball classes, practices, seasons, and camps.

FULL-COURT DRIBBLE WITH LAY-UPS

Stand behind the baseline. Dribble the length of the court as quickly as possible and finish with a full-speed, right-handed lay-up. On the way back down the court, dribble as quickly as possible using the left hand and finish with a full-speed, left-handed lay-up. Complete at least 10 repetitions with each hand. You can time yourself if desired. This is an effective drill for practicing full-speed dribbling and full-speed lay-ups.

REBOUND PASS TO OUTLET

One player—the rebounder—stands close to the basket (figure 9.6). The second player—the outlet man—stands at the three-point line at the top of the key. The rebounder taps the ball off the backboard, secures the rebound, and calls out "ball." Once the rebounder calls "ball," the outlet man cuts toward the sideline and calls "outlet." The rebounder should make a precise pass to the outlet. Once the outlet receives the ball, he or she dribbles the ball up the court as quickly as possible and shoots a lay-up at the far basket. The drill is repeated on the way back down the court, except the rebounder will serve as a trailer and will cut down the middle of the three-second lane to receive a pass from the outlet for a lay-up.

For variety, change the drill a little. Rather than tap the ball off the backboard, the rebounder tosses the ball up through the bottom of the net, simulating a made basket. The rebounder quickly steps out of bounds and delivers an accurate pass to the outlet close to the sideline. The remainder of the drill should be the same.

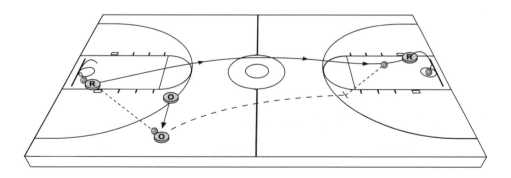

9.6 Rebound pass to outlet drill.

THREE-PLAYER WEAVE/2-ON-1 BACK

Players stand in three single-file lines behind a baseline (figure 9.7). The first person in the center line passes to the first person in the right line. The center player follows the pass, cutting behind the player on the right and gradually curling back to the middle of the court to receive an upcoming pass. The player on the right passes the ball to the first person in the left line, who has moved down the court to receive the pass. The player on the right follows the pass, cutting behind the player on the left and gradually curling back to the middle of the court to receive an upcoming pass. The player on the left passes the ball to the center player, who has curled back to the middle of the court. Players continue this process of weaving down the court (pass, follow the pass, cut behind, and curl back to the middle) as they approach the far basket. At the far basket, the player who receives a pass close to the basket should shoot a lay-up. After the shot is taken, the shooter sprints back to the original basket to play defense as the other two players bring the ball back down court, simulating a 2-on-1 fast break. This is an effective drill for practicing passing to moving targets, full-court lay-ups, and 2-on-1 fast breaks.

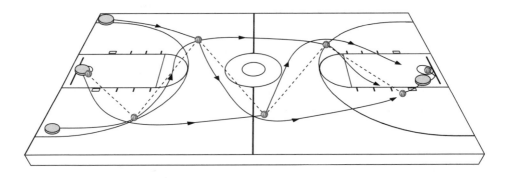

9.7   **Three-player weave/2-on-1 back drill.**

FIVE-PLAYER WEAVE/3-ON-2 BACK

Players stand in five single-file lines behind the baseline: right wing, right post, center, left post, and left wing (figure 9.8). After the center makes the initial pass to either one of the post players, the players use the same process of weaving (pass, follow the pass, cut behind, curl back to the middle) to move the ball down the court toward the far basket. At the far basket, one player (the assist man) passes to

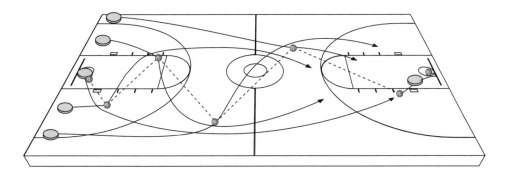

9.8 **Five-player weave/3-on-2 back drill.**

the player closest to the basket (the shooter), who shoots a lay-up. After the lay-up is taken, the shooter and assist man sprint back to play defense as the other three players bring the ball back down the court, simulating a 3-on-2 fast break. This is an effective drill for practicing passing to moving targets, full-court lay-ups, and 3-on-2 fast breaks.

INDIVIDUAL SKILLS TEST/SELF-TEST

You can use a variety of drills to test yourself on your skills. Develop a scoring system like the one shown in table 9.1 for the full-court dribble with lay-ups drill.

TECHNIQUE CHECKLISTS

Instructors and players can use a technique checklist to check for skill development on full-court offense fundamentals.

TABLE 9.1 FULL-COURT DRIBBLE WITH LAY-UPS: 60 SECONDS

10 or more	Hall-of-famer
8 to 9	MVP
6 to 7	All-star
4 to 5	Starter
0 to 3	Keep practicing

Full-Court Offense Fundamentals Checklist

_____ Clearly calls out "ball" and/or "outlet"

_____ Accurately passes to outlet

_____ Full-speed dribbling skills

_____ Full-court lay-up skills

_____ Accurately passes to moving targets

_____ Aggressively attacks the basket

_____ Fills the lane, keeps properly spaced

_____ Follows the initial shot, rebounds

Half-Court Offense

Half-court offense refers to the formations, plays, and sets used by an offensive team between the half-court line and the opponent's basket. The main objective of half-court offense is to produce the highest-percentage shot possible. Because only one offensive player can have possession of the basketball at any time, successful half-court offense depends on the productive play of the four offensive players who do not have possession of the ball. These players must be active and work together as an offensive unit. They must make the defense work by setting sound screens, making precise cuts, and helping teammates establish position as close to the basket as possible. These actions will help an offensive team achieve its main objective of producing as many high-quality shots as possible during a game.

During the 1990s, the NBA's Utah Jazz became famous for their effective half-court offense. With patience, persistence, and discipline, along with the use of precision screens, cuts, and passes, the Jazz were able to generate high-percentage scoring chances each game. Their half-court offense success resulted in the Utah Jazz being near the top in NBA team field-goal percentage on an annual basis. In addition, their half-court offense execution resulted in numerous victories for the franchise as they made the NBA playoffs every year during the 1990s.

The 3-2 and 1-4

There are a variety of half-court offensive formations that can be used. The type of offensive formation used by your team will probably depend on the characteristics and skills of the offensive players on your team as well as the type of defense an opponent is playing against you. The successful execution of each depends on the offensive players being well grounded in individual offensive skills, such as cutting, screening, passing, and shooting.

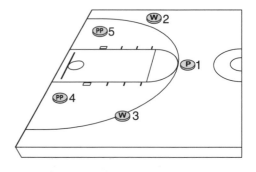

10.1　**The 3-2 half-court offense.**

The 3-2 half-court offense (figure 10.1) is probably the most common offensive formation used against a man-to-man defense. Also referred to as the 1-2-2 formation, the 3-2 half-court offense promotes passing, screening, cutting, and shooting by all five offensive players. The initial set includes the use of three perimeter players (a point and two wings) and two post players. The point is initially positioned beyond the top of the circle. The two wings are positioned around the three-point line, aligned with the free-throw line. The two post players are two to three steps from the baseline, halfway between the three-point line and the three-second lane.

Each player in a 3-2 offensive formation has a variety of options. For example, once the point initiates the half-court offense by passing the ball to either wing, the point can cut to the basket looking for a give-n-go pass from the wing, screen away for the opposite wing, set an on-the-ball screen for the wing, or set a down screen for either post player.

The advantage of half-court offense formations like the 3-2 is that they promote good spacing and inside/outside movement by all five players. Each player on the court, regardless of size or natural position, will have a chance to work back and forth from the perimeter to the post as the offensive team tries to produce the best shot possible. All five offensive players will have a chance to touch the ball and try to create offensive opportunities.

The 1-4 half-court offense (figure 10.2) is another common offensive formation used against a man-to-man defense. Like the 3-2 offensive set, the 1-4 promotes passing, screening, cutting, and shooting by all five offensive players on the court. The initial set includes the use of three perimeter players (a point and two wings) and two post players. The point is initially positioned beyond the

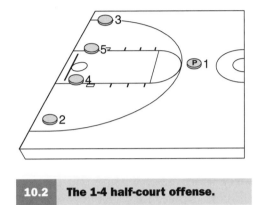

10.2 **The 1-4 half-court offense.**

top of the circle. The two wings are usually positioned just inside the three-point line and close to the baseline. The two post players are usually positioned just outside the three-second lane and close to the baseline. The typical 1-4 offensive uses a variety of back screens and down screens to help offensive players make cuts toward the basket and the ball.

The 1-4 offensive set is usually set into motion when the point dribbles to a free-throw line elbow. The post player on the opposite side of the court of the chosen elbow will cut to the other free-throw line elbow to receive a pass from the point. The post player on the same side of the court as the point will set a back screen for the close wing player. The wing player will use the back screen and cut toward the basketball, looking for a pass from the post player with the ball. If the wing player does not receive a pass, he or she continues through the three-second lane and fills the position by the block vacated by the post player who has the ball. The point will now set a down screen for the post player who set a back screen. The post player will use the down screen and cut up to the free-throw line elbow just vacated by the point. The post player with the ball will pass to the post player who just cut to the free-throw line elbow. The screens, cuts, and ball movement continue until a high-percentage shot is created by the offense.

The Double Low Post   The double low post (figure 10.3) is another
common offensive formation that
promotes the use of cutting, screening, passing, and shooting by all five
players on the court. Typically used
against a man-to-man defense, the
double low post may be a good formation to use when an offensive team
possesses two skilled post players.
The player formation for the double
low post is similar to the 3-2 offensive
formation, except that the two post

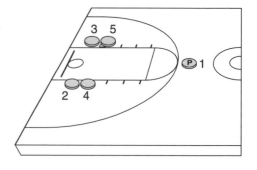

10.3	The double low post.

players (power forward and center) are positioned down low on either
side of the basket rather than between the three-second lane and
the three-point line. The point guard is initially positioned beyond
the top of the circle and the two wing players are positioned around
the three-point line, aligned with the free-throw line.

   Although each offensive player in the double low post has a variety
of options, the strength of the double low post is that with two skilled
inside players, the three perimeter players can constantly look to
pass the basketball into the post area. Numerous high-percentage
shots can be created if the two skilled post players can frequently
receive the basketball close to the basket. The emphasis on utilizing
the strong inside players can also help generate free-throw shooting
opportunities for the offense and foul trouble for the defense. Because
the two best inside players are already positioned near the basket,
the double low post can also be effective for offensive rebounding.

Screen Away—Cut Toward   One of the most important prin-
ciples of half-court offense, regardless of formation, is movement
without the basketball. The four offensive players who do not have
the ball must move on offense to make things happen rather than
just watch the player with the basketball. These four players must
not only move, they must move with purpose—move to open areas
on the court to receive a pass or move toward a defender to set a
screen for a teammate. Moving with purpose on offense increases
the defensive challenge for the opponent and increases the number
of high-quality scoring opportunities.

   One of the most basic concepts associated with the principle of
movement without the basketball is referred to as screen away-cut
toward (figure 10.4). An offensive player positioned close to the basketball should cut away from the ball and set a screen for a teammate positioned away from the ball (screen away). Once the screen

is set, the teammate positioned away from the basketball should use the screen and aggressively cut toward the ball or toward the basket. If the player with the ball is patient and allows this process to take place, he or she will be able to deliver an accurate pass to the cutter, who should have a good chance to shoot and score. This type of offensive movement must be continuous until a high-percentage shot is produced by the offense.

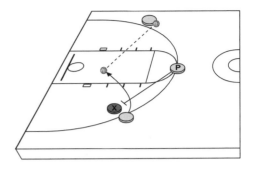

10.4 **Screen away—cut toward.**

Types of Cuts Cutting is another fundamental principle of half-court offense. Typically cuts are used by offensive players to move closer to the basket (inside), move toward the ball, or move toward perimeter spots on the court (outside). The offensive player using the cut must be precise when making the cut so that he can quickly create space between himself and the defender in order to receive the basketball. Common cuts used in a half-court offense include the V-cut, the curl cut, the pivot cut, and the backdoor cut.

The V-cut (figure 10.5) is used to divert a defender away from the direction an offensive player actually wants to move. It is also used to create space between a defender playing aggressively so that an

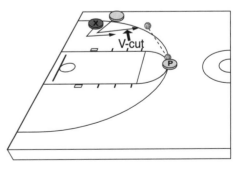

10.5 **V-cut.**

offensive player can receive the basketball. To attempt a V-cut, first take two to three steps in the direction away from where you will actually cut. After the last step, quickly push off the ground using the planted foot and cut sharply back toward your original position on the court. As you move back to your original position, create a target with your hands in preparation of receiving a pass from your teammate.

The curl cut (figure 10.6) is an inside cut often used by players immediately after an interior screen is set. To attempt a curl cut, first allow the interior screen to be set. After the screen is set, cut in a curved path around the screener toward the basketball. Create a target with your hands as you cut, preparing to receive a pass from your teammate.

The pivot cut (figure 10.7) is an inside cut often employed by post players. The pivot cut helps players establish effective post position against a defender. To attempt a pivot cut, first move toward the post defender and plant a foot close to the defender. Pivot on the planted foot to establish post position. This movement will pin the defender behind you. Your back will be toward the defender, and you should be able to see the player with the ball. Extend a target hand in preparation to receive a pass from your teammate.

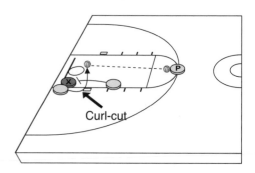

Curl-cut

10.6   **Curl cut.**

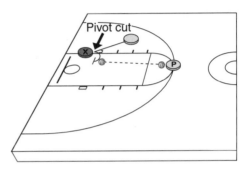

| 10.7 | Pivot cut. |

A backdoor cut (figure 10.8) is an effective perimeter cut to use when a defender is overplaying defense against an offensive player or when the defender loses sight of the basketball. To attempt a backdoor cut, establish an initial perimeter position. If you suspect that the defender is overplaying you on defense, take a quick jab step away from the basket. If the defender follows you in that direction, quickly push off on the foot you used for the jab step and cut toward the basket. If you have created space between you and the defender, you should be open for a pass from a teammate, followed by an inside shot close to the basket.

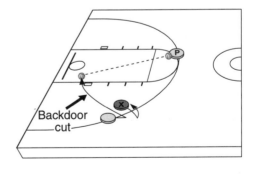

| 10.8 | Backdoor cut. |

Spacing on the Court Another essential element of half-court offense is on-court spacing among teammates (figure 10.9). Offensive players must stay properly spaced on the court so that one defender cannot guard more than one offensive player at a time. For example, if two offensive players are positioned too close together in the three-second lane, only one defensive player is needed to defend both players and the basket. Improper spacing on the court may eliminate good passing angles between teammates and potential gaps in the defense for offensive teammates to penetrate. Keeping the middle of the court open will also provide offensive players space to cut toward that area to receive the basketball.

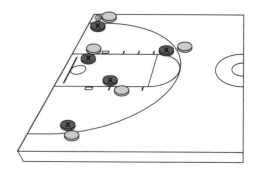

10.9 Proper spacing.

Zone Offense Various types of offensive formations can be used to attack a half-court zone defense. The following rules will lead to offensive success, regardless of the type of zone defense the opponent is using. First, to better confront the defensive formation, the offense should use the front opposite the one the zone defense is using. For example, if the zone defense is using an odd-front formation (1-2-2 or 3-2), the offensive team should use an even-front formation (2-1-2) to confront and attack the zone (figure 10.10).

Zone Offense

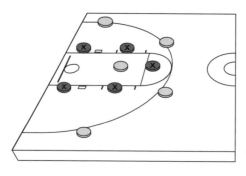
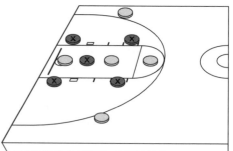

10.10 a. 1-2-2 zone.   b. 2-1-2 zone.

Second, offensive players must penetrate the gaps—the spaces between zone defenders—in the zone defense with dribble-drives and cuts. Third, offensive players must move into open spaces and seams in the zone defense, especially to the middle of the three-second lane, looking for passes from teammates. Fourth, offensive players must use quick passes and ball reversals to make the zone defenders move and work. Making zone defenders move will help create gaps in the defense for offensive players to penetrate using dribble-drives and cuts.

Position Responsibilities

In a game, the success of a half-court offense greatly depends on the productivity of the offensive players who do not have the basketball. Through effective interactions with teammates using precise screens and cuts, the four players without the basketball can help generate a high-percentage shot for one of their teammates.

The point guard should initiate the use of a half-court offensive formation by yelling out verbal instructions to teammates, such as "3-2," "1-4," or "motion," whatever term the team uses to initiates the use of a specific half-court offensive formation. If the 3-2 formation is used, a pass to the wing or another common initiating option immediately follows the point's instruction. Once the pass is made to the wing, the point will typically screen away for the opposite wing or post player or cut to the basket looking for the quick give-n-go pass from the wing. If the point cuts through the lane without receiving a pass, he or she should continue to the other side of the court to balance the player positions on the court.

The wing player should use a V-cut to shed the defender and receive the basketball from the point. If the defense is overplaying, the wing should use a backdoor cut to the basket. When the wing receives the basketball, he or she should assume the triple-threat position and look to take an immediate jump shot (catch-n-shoot). If a shot within the wing's shooting range is unavailable, the wing should look to dribble-drive to the basket, possibly with the help of a screen by the post player on the same side of the court. If no dribble-drive is available, the wing should look for a pass to the near post player or for a swing pass to the other wing. If the pass to the post is available, the wing should immediately spot up on the three-point line if the post kicks the ball back to the wing for a shot. When the ball is on the other side of the court, the wing should set down screens for post players or spot up around the three-point line in preparation for a swing pass from the other wing player.

The post player on the same side of the court as the ball should immediately use the pivot cut to establish post position and look for a pass from the point. If the post doesn't receive a pass after a one-second count, he or she should screen away for the opposite post. The post should look to set back screens for the wing player on the nonball side of the court so that the wing can cut toward the middle of the court to receive a pass.

WING V-CUT

Start in a wing position on the court. Practice using a V-cut before receiving a pass from the point (played by a teacher, coach, or teammate). Focus on initial position on the court, as well as the precise footwork necessary to shed a defender.

Once you have confidence in your footwork and technique, add a defender. Focus on shedding the defender with a V-cut and successfully receiving the pass from the point. To practice a backdoor cut, have the defender overplay on defense and then use a jab step to initiate the cut.

WING V-CUT PLUS CATCH-N-SHOOT

Divide players into partners. One player starts in a wing position on the court; the other player serves as the point. The wing player practices using the V-cut and the catch-n-shoot together. Focus on footwork, squaring the body and feet to the basket, and on shooting mechanics to promote success.

You can add a third player as a wing defender to make the practice more gamelike. Have the defender gradually increase defensive intensity as the wing player develops confidence. Rotate positions after every five practice trials.

TWO-MAN POST GAME

Divide players into groups of five (figure 10.11). One player is the point, two players are wings, and two players are posts. Perimeter players will pass the ball around the perimeter. Post players practice the one-second count when the ball is on their side of the court before they screen away for the opposite post. Wing

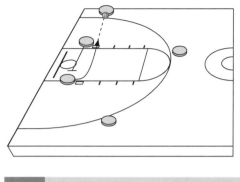

10.11 Two-man post game setup.

players should occasionally pass the ball into the post for an inside shot. The focus of the drill is timing for post players.

POST KICK-OUT

Divide players into groups of four (figure 10.12). One player is the wing, one is the post, and the other two are defenders. After the wing passes to the post, he or she should spot up behind the three-point line for a jump shot. As the defenders double-team the post, the post practices the timing of the kick-out pass to the wing, who will catch-n-shoot the ball for a three-point shot. Focus should

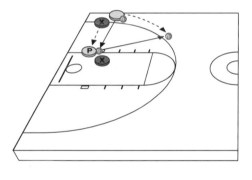

10.12 Post kick-out drill.

be on player spacing and the timing of the kick-out to the wing.

5-ON-5 WITHOUT DRIBBLING

Divide players into groups of five and assign two groups to each basket. One group starts on offense, the other on defense. The offense tries to produce a high-percentage shot without any dribbling. The offense can shoot only from inside the three-second lane. Emphasize the half-court offense principle of screen away—cut toward. If the offense shoots outside the three-second lane, the drill is temporarily paused and the five offensive players must complete 5 to 10 jumping jacks, knee-highs, or other conditioning activity. If the offense scores a basket on a lay-up, all five defenders must complete a similar conditioning activity.

PENETRATE ZONE GAPS

Divide players into groups of five and assign two groups to each basket. One group starts on offense, the other on defense. The defense uses a half-court zone defense such as the 2-3 zone or 3-2 zone. The offense tries to penetrate the gaps of the zone through the use of quick ball reversals and dribble-drives. The offensive goal is to make an inside shot within five feet of the basket. If the offense accomplishes this goal, the drill is temporarily paused and the five defensive players must complete 5 to 10 jumping jacks, knee-highs, or other conditioning activity. If the defense does not allow a made basket during a one-minute practice period, the offensive players must complete a similar conditioning task.

TECHNIQUE CHECKLISTS

Instructors and players can use technique checklists to check for skill development on specific or general half-court offense fundamentals.

General Half-Court Offense Technique Checklist

_____ Maintain communication with teammates

_____ Maintain proper spacing and court balance

_____ Keep the middle of the court open

_____ Move to a vacated spot quickly

_____ Use the triple-threat position each ball possession

_____ Use basic cuts effectively

Movement and Cuts Technique Checklist

_____ Effective use of V-cut

_____ Effective use of curl cut

_____ Effective use of pivot cut

_____ Effective use of backdoor cut

Inbounding the Ball

During a basketball season, the outcome of many games at each level of competition is decided by how effectively (or ineffectively) a team inbounds the ball. Successful inbounding helps a team maintain ball possession and promotes scoring opportunities. Unsuccessful inbounding may cause unnecessary turnovers for a team, often leading to more scoring opportunities for the opponent.

Executing the Inbounds Pass

The main objective of most inbounds plays is for the offense to maintain possession of the basketball. However, the objective of some inbounds plays may be to create an immediate scoring opportunity from the inbounds pass. Regardless of the objective, all five players on a team must use basic basketball fundamentals, such as screens, cuts, and passes, to successfully execute an inbounds play. The failure by even one offensive player to do so may result in a turnover at a crucial moment in the game.

When you are called on to pass the ball inbounds, you first must establish legal position out of bounds (figure 11.1a). The ball and all body parts, including feet and shoes, may not be in contact with the basketball court or even the lines of the basketball court. You must establish position behind the sideline or baseline. If your shoes contact the sideline or baseline before you release the basketball, a violation will be called and possession of the ball will be given to the other team. Another important consideration when inbounding from the baseline is the backboard. Establish position far enough away from the backboard so that the structure will not interfere with the inbounds pass.

Once properly positioned out of bounds, behind either the baseline or sideline, execute the proper fundamentals for the inbounds play. Communicate clearly with your teammates, loudly calling out the chosen inbounds play. Use a ball slap to initiate the execution of the inbounds play (figure 11.1b). When the players on the court hear the slap, they begin executing the play.

If a defender is trying to deny the inbounds pass, use pass fakes to cause the defender to move in the opposite direction of where the ball needs to be passed. As the inbounds play develops, recognize

11.1   **a. Legal position out of bounds.**

the best passing option and quickly react by using the appropriate pass (chest pass, bounce pass, overhead pass, etc.) to successfully deliver the basketball to your teammate on the court (figure 11.1c).

For a team to successfully inbound the basketball, all five players—not just the inbounder—must complete their responsibilities. The four players on the court should listen carefully to the inbounder as the play is called out. Once the play is called, they should quickly line up in the proper formation to execute the play. They need to listen and watch for the inbounder to initiate the play with a ball slap. Once the play is initiated, they need to use precise cuts and screens to properly execute the play in order to achieve the desired objective.

b. Slap the ball to begin the play.

c. Pass to a teammate inbounds.

Basic inbounds play formations include the line, the box, and the T. All three formations provide a variety of potential screening options for an offensive team. Regardless of formation or movement patterns used with each inbounds play, the main objective is to create a situation in which a teammate can cut to the basket, to an open area on the court, or toward the inbounder to receive a pass in order to maintain ball possession and sometimes produce a quick scoring opportunity.

Box Formation The box formation (figure 11.2) is a common player arrangement to use when inbounding the basketball. The court positions of four offensive players form a box or square. This formation promotes the use of screens and cuts to produce open shots and passing lanes.

Box

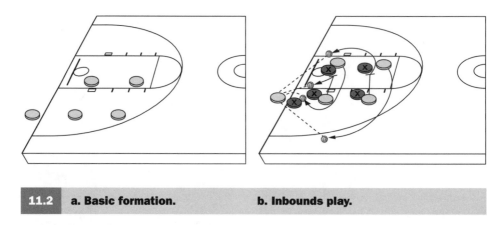

| 11.2 | a. Basic formation. | b. Inbounds play. |

The box formation is created by positioning two offensive players by the free-throw line elbows and two offensive players close to the basket, just outside the three-second lane. The location of the box on the court can be adjusted to match the position of the offensive player inbounding the basketball.

A typical box formation inbounds play calls for two offensive players (usually the two positioned closest to the inbounder) to screen away from two offensive players positioned farther away so that at least two players are cutting toward the basketball. The movement of the screeners can also be lateral (left or right) depending on the position of the inbounder and the objective of the inbounds play.

Line Formation The line formation (figure 11.3) is another common player arrangement used by an offensive team when inbounding the basketball. It can be an effective formation to use from the baseline when looking to create a quick "pass-catch-shoot" opportunity close to the basket.

Line

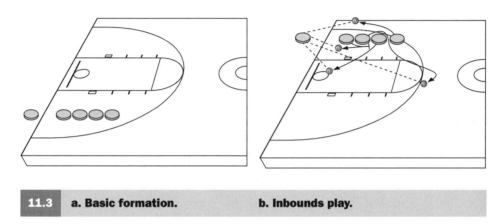

| 11.3 | a. Basic formation. | b. Inbounds play. |

The typical line formation calls for the offensive players on the court to form a straight line directly across from the inbounder. On the slap of the basketball by the inbounder, players in the line make quick cuts to different spots on the court looking for a quick pass, or a quick catch-n-shoot chance (like an alley-oop play). If a quick pass close to the basket is not possible, the offensive players continue to move to open areas on the court so that the ball can be passed inbounds and ball possession retained before a five-second violation occurs.

T Formation The T formation (figure 11.4) is another common player arrangement used by an offensive team when inbounding the basketball. Similar to the box formation, offensive players are initially spaced apart on the court to create screening and cutting opportunities toward the player inbounding the basketball. The typical T formation is created by positioning one player in the middle of the three-second lane, close to the basket. A second player is positioned in the middle of the free-throw line. Two other offensive players are positioned as wing players on each side of the court around the three-point line. On the slap of the ball by the inbounder, at least one offensive player (usually the player in the three-second lane) will screen away from the basketball for a teammate (usually a wing player) so that an offensive player can make a precise cut toward the inbounder.

T Formation

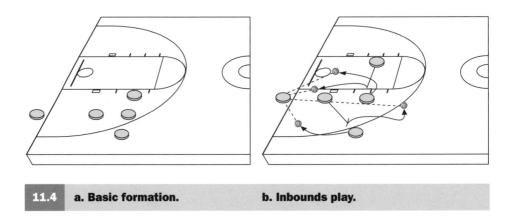

| **11.4** | **a. Basic formation.** | **b. Inbounds play.** |

Inbounding From the Sideline Versus the Baseline   The line, box, and T formations can be used from either the sideline or baseline. Depending on how close you are to your opponent's basket when passing the ball inbounds, your opponent may or may not challenge the inbounds pass. For example, when the inbounder is positioned under the opponent's basket, the opponent usually will defend the inbounds pass very aggressively, trying to deny a quick scoring opportunity and produce a turnover. The scenario may be the exact opposite when inbounding the ball from the sideline far away from the opponent's basket. In this situation, the opponent will probably not defend or contest the inbounds pass. This makes it very easy to maintain ball possession for the offensive team.

Take it to the court

The Inbounder

At numerous points during a basketball game, each team will be required to inbound the ball. Before a basketball team even participates in a game, the teacher or coach needs to identify which players will serve as the inbounders. A taller player on the team is usually chosen because he or she can see the whole court and will have a better chance of passing the ball over a player trying to deny the inbounds pass. The player who inbounds the ball must be positioned at the point where the ball crossed over the sideline or baseline and went out of bounds. The coach usually communicates with the inbounder about which play to use, and the inbounder then communicates the chosen play to his or her teammates on the court.

Once the game official hands the basketball to the inbounder, the offense has five seconds to successfully pass the ball inbounds. The four players on the court must use precise screens and cuts to shed their defenders in order to become open to receive the inbounds pass. In many situations, an offensive player may first serve as a screener for a teammate and then become a cutter, moving quickly toward the basket or inbounder after the screen is set. Sometimes the inbounder shoots the ball if it is returned after the inbounder reenters the court. Once the ball is successfully passed inbounds, the offensive team may be able to score immediately from the pass or transition directly into a half-court offensive play or set.

When the defense is aggressively denying the inbounds pass, the inbounder is responsible for calling a timeout before five seconds has expired if he or she is unable to inbound the ball. The inbounder must know exactly how many timeouts his or her team has in case this scenario develops. If the offense is unable to pass the ball inbounds but has no timeouts to use (or does not want to use a timeout to maintain ball possession), a five-second violation is called and the defense gains possession of the basketball.

For most inbounding situations, the player passing the ball inbounds cannot move from his or her initial position because the inbounder has to be stationary at the point where the basketball went out of bounds. However, after a made basket by the opponent, the inbounder can move anywhere along the baseline to pass the ball inbounds to a teammate.

Give it a go: Inbounding

PARTNER INBOUNDING

The inbounder gets into position behind the baseline (figure 11.5). The other player cuts to different spots on the floor to receive the inbounds pass. The inbounder should practice using different passes to inbound the ball to the moving target.

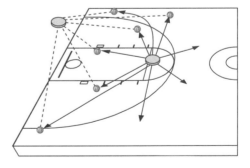

11.5 Partner inbounding drill.

Add a defender on the inbounder to increase the challenge of passing the ball inbounds. The inbounder should use different passes and pass fakes if necessary to successfully inbound the ball to the moving target. Alternate player positions after every three to five practice trials.

FIVE-SECOND DRILL

Divide players into groups of five and assign each group to a basket (figure 11.6). Two players are on offense (inbounder and cutter), two players are on defense (denying the inbounds pass and defending the cutter), and one player is the official. The inbounder stands behind either the baseline or the sideline. Once the official gives the inbounder the ball, the inbounder has five seconds to successfully pass the ball to the cutter. The inbounder should initiate the play with a ball slap. If the defense doesn't allow an inbounds pass in five seconds or steals the inbounds pass, the offensive players must complete 10 jumping jacks, knee-highs, or other conditioning activity. If the offense is able to successfully inbound the ball three consecutive times, the defense must complete the conditioning task. Alternate player positions after four to six practice trials. Gradually add one more defender and offensive player to each group to make the drill more gamelike.

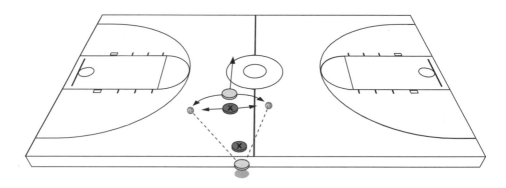

11.6   **Five-second drill setup.**

INBOUNDS PLAY CREATION/EXECUTION

Divide players into teams of five. Assign two teams to each basket. Each team creates two inbounds plays for the sideline and two inbounds plays for the baseline using the basic play formations (box, line, and T). After the plays have been created, give each team's players five minutes to practice the plays without the other team's players seeing them practice. After each team practices, the players try to execute their inbounds plays against each other. The team on defense should use aggressive man-to-man defense to deny the inbounds pass. If either team is able to score directly off an inbounds play, the other team must immediately complete 10 jumping jacks, knee-highs, or other conditioning activity.

TECHNIQUE CHECKLISTS

Instructors and players can use this technique checklist to check for skill development on specific or general inbounding fundamentals.

Inbounding the Ball Technique Checklist

_____ Safely position out of bounds, away from backboard
_____ Clearly and loudly call out inbounds play
_____ Initiate the play with a ball slap
_____ Use a pass fake, if necessary, to pass ball inbounds
_____ Use the appropriate pass (chest, bounce, overhead, etc.)
_____ Make pass accurate and catchable

Team Defense

The adage "defense wins championships" has been used for years in all types of competitive sport situations. The statement still has relevance today, especially with the game of basketball. Although an offensively-minded team is usually exciting to watch and gains fan support, defense-oriented teams typically bring home championship trophies because they are able to dictate the number of good scoring chances their opponent has during a game. Overall success on defense depends on each defender being well grounded in individual defensive fundamentals, being physically fit, and having a high level of athleticism. All five defenders on the court must work together toward one common goal: not allowing the opponent to score.

The NBA's Detroit Pistons once exemplified what superior team defense can accomplish. The Pistons used aggressive, physical defensive play to intimidate and shut down the most potent offensive teams and players of the late 1980s. They made opponents work extremely hard for every shot, and rarely gave up an easy basket. Pistons games were typically low scoring, as opponents' field goal percentage was below average and turnover count was high. Labeled the "Bad Boys" by the national media and powered by a unified team defense, Detroit won back-to-back NBA championships, solidifying its position as one of the great defensive teams in NBA history.

Man-to-Man Defense

The most common type of team defense used in basketball is man-to-man defense (figure 12.1). Man-to-man defense requires each defender to guard or match up against an offensive player. The defender must shadow the offensive player wherever he or she moves on the court, always staying between the basket and the offensive player.

The defender's primary responsibility is not to allow the offensive player to dribble-drive to the basket or complete a wide-open jump shot.

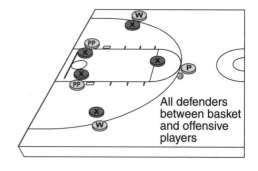

All defenders between basket and offensive players

12.1 Man-to-man defensive positions on the court.

In man-to-man defense, defenders are usually matched with offensive players on the basis of comparable speed, position, height, and ability. For example, a team's best perimeter defender will probably be matched against the opponent's best perimeter scoring threat.

In man-to-man team defense, all five defenders must strive to protect their basket at all times, regardless of where the offensive player they are guarding moves on the court. The challenge of protecting the basket starts with applying defensive pressure on the player who has the basketball (point), making it difficult for this player to dribble, pass, or shoot.

Always try to push the basketball away from the middle of the three-second lane. Force the basketball toward the sidelines. A defense breaks down quickly once the offense is able to move the basketball to the middle of the three-second lane. Minimize second-chance shots by boxing out the offensive player and rebounding the ball.

Always be in position so that you can see where the opponent is you are guarding and where the basketball is. By doing so, you will be able to move over and provide help on defense if a teammate gets beat to the basket by the player with the basketball. This is called help-side defense—providing defensive help to teammates who have been beaten to the basket by the offensive player.

Depending on the position of the basketball on the court, each man-to-man defender must continually adjust position on the court in order to see the basketball and the offensive player. This will allow each defender to recognize and react to situations in which help-side defense is necessary. When defensive help is needed, defenders must quickly move or slide to a position between the basket and the offensive player dribble-driving to the basket in order to deny an easy inside shot. Help-side defense positioning depends on how many passes away—one, two, or three—a defender is from the basketball (figure 12.2). The proper help-side defensive position for each situation allows the defender to see the ball and the offensive player being guarded.

Handle screens consistently. Always determine how you will handle offensive screens before the start of the game—switching on screens with other defenders or fighting through screens to stay with the offensive player you are guarding—and then stick with the plan. Always communicate with other defenders in order to effectively adapt to defensive situations and needs. Call out "shot," "help," "switch," or "screen" as necessary to make your teammates aware of immediate defensive situations during a game.

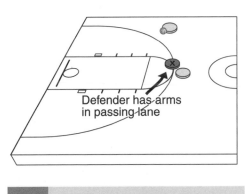

Defender has arms in passing lane

12.2 **a. Defender one pass away.**

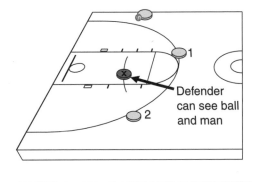

Defender can see ball and man

12.2 **b. Defender two passes away.**

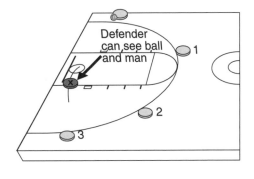

Defender can see ball and man

12.2 **c. Defender three passes away.**

Zone Defense   Another common type of team defense is zone defense (figure 12.3). With a zone defense, each defender is assigned to a particular area or region of the court rather than to a specific offensive player. A zone defender's primary responsibility is to prevent the opponent from scoring in his or her assigned area. When the basketball enters the defender's region of the court, he or she must use man-to-man defensive fundamentals to deny the offensive player a dribble-drive to the basket or an open jump shot.

Zone Defenses

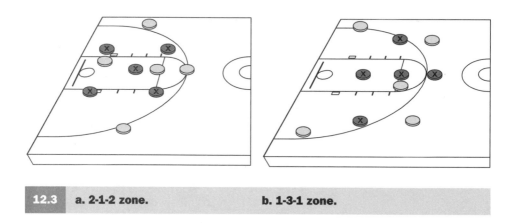

| 12.3 | a. 2-1-2 zone. | b. 1-3-1 zone. |

Two common types of zone defenses are the 2-1-2 and 1-3-1. A defensive team may use the 2-1-2 zone against an opponent with strong inside players. The 2-1-2 zone places two defenders on the blocks, one defender in the middle of the three-second lane, and two defenders on the free-throw line elbows. A key advantage of the 2-1-2 zone is that it positions more defenders close to the basket. Having more defenders close to the basket will help the defensive team defend against strong inside players, and with defensive rebounding. A disadvantage of the 2-1-2 is that it may allow opponents more open perimeter jump shots, especially three-point shots.

The 1-3-1 is an excellent zone defense to use to create trapping situations and turnovers. It can also be a very useful defensive formation for a team with long-armed, athletic defenders. The 1-3-1 zone places a back defender in the three-second lane close to the basket, a defender at the middle of the free-throw line, a wing defender on both sides of the middle defender, and a point defender just beyond the top of the key. The objective of the 1-3-1 is to force the offense to move the basketball toward the sidelines in order to create a trap, especially in the corners where the baseline and sidelines intersect. The point defender must try to push the offensive player with the basketball toward the sideline. Once the ball has been pushed to the sideline, the closest two defenders (usually a wing defender and point defender) set the trap on the offensive player with the ball. The other defenders eliminate passing lanes by positioning themselves between the offensive player with the ball and the closest offensive players. Effective traps help produce jump-ball situations and turnovers for the defense. A disadvantage of the 1-3-1 is that if the trap is not successfully created, the offensive player with the ball may be able to step or dribble through the trapping defenders and successfully pass to an offensive player positioned close to the basket.

When using a zone defense, assume the basic defensive stance when in your assigned region of the court. This will help you quickly adjust to ball position and will help deny dribble penetration into the zone. Keep your eyes on the basketball; never lose sight of it! Zone defenders must quickly and constantly adjust their defensive positioning so that they can see where the basketball is on the court. Defend the three-second lane by eliminating passing lanes into the middle of the zone. Force the offense to pass the basketball around the perimeter. Just as with a man-to-man team defense, a zone defense quickly breaks down once the offense moves the ball into the middle of the zone. Keep your arms extended to minimize access to passing lanes. A long, extended arm will help you get your fingertips on passes, often resulting in turnovers. Communicate with other defenders in order to adjust to zone defensive situations. Use terms such as "cutter middle," "cutter low," "cutter high," "shot," "help," and "screen" to make teammates aware of defensive situations during a game.

Combination Defenses Elements of man-to-man defense and zone defense can be combined to form what is referred to as combination defense (figure 12.4). Combination defenses usually are short-term strategies used to combat an opponent's specific offensive strengths. The most common combination defenses are the box-and-1 and the triangle-and-2.

Combination Defenses

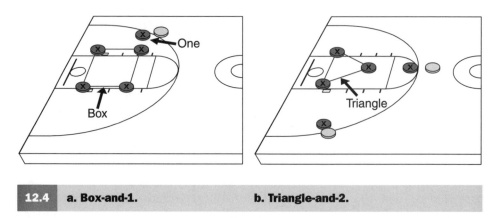

| 12.4 | a. Box-and-1. | b. Triangle-and-2. |

The box-and-1 is typically used against an opponent who has one main scoring threat. Four defenders form a box or square around the edges of the three-second lane, while the fifth defender matches up in man-to-man defense against the opponent's main offensive player. This defender shadows the main offensive player wherever he or she moves on the court, trying to minimize the number of good looks and shots for that player. The other four defenders cover their regions of the court and help out defensively whenever the main offensive player enters their regions with the basketball.

The triangle-and-2 is typically used against an opponent who has two main scoring threats. Three defenders form a zone triangle inside the three-second lane to protect the basket while two players match up in man-to-man defense against the two scoring threats. The two man-to-man defenders shadow the two main offensive threats wherever they move on the court. The other three defenders cover their regions of the court and help out defensively when the main offensive threats enter their regions with the basketball.

Pressing Defenses   Basic man-to-man and zone defenses can be extended to a half-court, three-quarters court, and full-court formation. This adjustment usually is made to make it more difficult for the offensive team to advance the ball up the court. Therefore, these defenses are typically referred to as pressing defenses (figure 12.5). The main objective of a press is to create an offensive turnover in the form of a bad pass or 10-second violation, both of which will give the ball back to the defensive team. Defensive teams often use presses against opponents who are not skilled at ball handling or when the defensive team is behind in the game.

Pressing Defenses

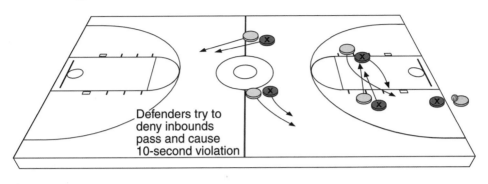

Defenders try to deny inbounds pass and cause 10-second violation

| 12.5 | a. Full-court man-to-man press. |

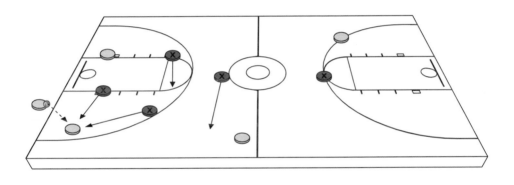

| 12.5 | b. 1-2-1-1 zone press. |

Two common pressing defenses are the full-court, man-to-man press and the 1-2-1-1 zone press. The full-court man-to-man press requires each defender to match up and shadow an offensive player for the entire length of the basketball court. Defenders try to deny the pass to the offensive players they are guarding as well as to deny the dribble up the court. In the 1-2-1-1 zone press, the defense tries to create a turnover by encouraging the opponent to inbound a pass toward the corners and sidelines of the court, then trapping the offensive player with the basketball. An effective trap may cause the defender to make an errant pass, lose control of the basketball, or force him or her to call a timeout, all acceptable outcomes for the defensive team.

Choosing a Defense

In a game situation, a team should use the type of defense that best utilizes its players' abilities and matches up with the characteristics of the opposition. Generally speaking, a man-to-man defense should be used if your team matches up well physically and athletically with the opponent or if your opponent is a good outside-shooting team. A zone defense may be effective against an opponent that has strong, skilled post players. Positioning more defenders close to the basket in a zone defense will make it more difficult for the opponent's post players to receive the basketball. A pressing defense might be effective against an opponent that lacks good dribblers and ball-handlers or if your team has superior athleticism and conditioning. A pressing defense also can be very effective after your team makes a field goal or free throw. A full-court press often surprises, and even confuses, an unprepared offense into making a turnover. In any case, if an opponent is scoring easy baskets against the type of defense you are using, quickly change to a different type of defense to keep your opponent off balance and make it more difficult for the team to score.

Give it a go: Team Defense

HELP-SIDE D

Divide players into teams of five. Assign two groups to each basket; one team plays offense, the other plays man-to-man defense. The five defenders match up with offensive players of equal size and ability. As the five offensive players pass the basketball around the perimeter, the five defensive players adjust their defensive positioning to the court position of the ball, depending on whether they are one, two, or three passes away from the basketball. After everyone is accustomed to the drill, the offense begins to attack the basket. Switch offense to defense and defense to offense after three to five minutes.

60-SECOND ZONE

Divide players into teams of five. One team plays offense, the other plays defense. The defense uses a traditional half-court zone defense such as the 2-1-2 or 1-3-1. The offense has 60 seconds to try to make as many baskets as possible against the zone. Offensive players should focus on ball movement, penetrating the zone with dribble-drives, and passing the basketball into the middle of the three-second lane. The defense should focus on denying passing lanes into the middle of the zone and creating turnovers. After 60 seconds, compare the number of baskets made by the offense to the number of turnovers or violations created by the defense. If the offense made more baskets, the five defenders must complete 10 jumping jacks, knee-highs, or other conditioning activity. If the defense produced more turnovers or violations, the offense must complete the conditioning task. Switch offense to defense and vice versa every three to five minutes.

FULL-COURT PRESS

Divide players into teams of five. Assign two groups to each full court. One team plays offense, the other plays defense. The defensive team uses a full-court, man-to-man press. Assign one offensive player to inbound the ball after a simulated made basket. The five offensive players try to advance the ball up the court against the man-to-man press. After a few minutes, compare the number of baskets made by the offense to the number of turnovers or violations created by the defense. If the offense was able to make more baskets, all five defenders must complete 10 jumping jacks, knee-highs, or other conditioning activity. If the defense produced more turnovers or violations, the offense must complete the conditioning task. Switch offense to defense and defense to offense after five to seven minutes.

SWITCH

Divide players into teams of five (figure 12.6). Assign two groups to each basket. One team plays offense, the other plays man-to-man defense. Create a 5-on-5, half-court offensive situation. The defenders should focus on calling out screens and switching as the offensive players run a freelance, motion offense using a variety of screens and cuts.

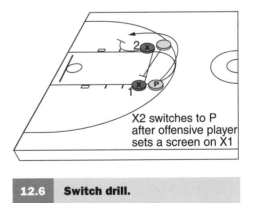

X2 switches to P after offensive player sets a screen on X1

12.6 Switch drill.

TECHNIQUE CHECKLISTS

Instructors and players can use this technique checklist to check for skill development on specific or general inbounding fundamentals.

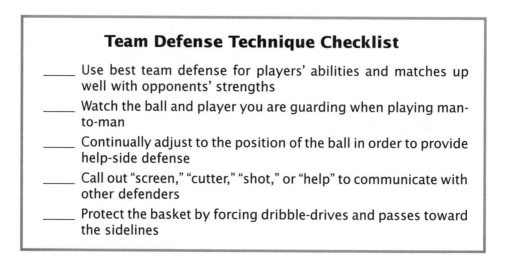

Team Defense Technique Checklist

_____ Use best team defense for players' abilities and matches up well with opponents' strengths

_____ Watch the ball and player you are guarding when playing man-to-man

_____ Continually adjust to the position of the ball in order to provide help-side defense

_____ Call out "screen," "cutter," "shot," or "help" to communicate with other defenders

_____ Protect the basket by forcing dribble-drives and passes toward the sidelines

About the Writer

Jon Oliver is an assistant professor of physical education at Eastern Illinois University in Charleston, Illinois, where he teaches beginning and intermediate basketball classes. After playing high school basketball in Indiana, Oliver accumulated a broad range of basketball teaching experience at the educational, recreational, and competitive levels. He has served as a basketball class instructor, high school coach, youth instructor, and summer basketball camp coach. Oliver is a graduate of Brigham Young University and earned his PhD from the University of Kansas in 2002.

Sports Fundamentals Series

Learning sports basics has never been more effective—or more fun—than with the new Sports Fundamentals Series. These books enable recreational athletes to engage in the activity quickly. Quick participation, not hours of reading, makes learning more fun and more effective.

Each chapter addresses a specific skill for that particular sport, leading the athlete through a simple, four-step sequence:

- *You Can Do It:* The skill is introduced with sequential instructions and accompanying photographs.

- *More to Choose and Use:* Variations and extensions of the primary skill are covered.

- *Take It to the Court/Field:* Readers learn how to apply the skill in competition.

- *Give It a Go:* These provide several direct experiences for gauging, developing, and honing the skill.

The writers of the Sports Fundamentals Series books are veteran instructors and coaches with extensive knowledge of their sport. They communicate clearly and succinctly, making reading and applying the content to the sport enjoyable for both younger and older recreational athletes. And with books on more and more sports being developed, you're sure to get up to speed quickly on any sport you want to play.

The Sports Fundamentals Series will include:

- Soccer
- Basketball
- Golf
- Softball
- Weight Training
- Bowling
- Archery
- Tennis
- Volleyball
- Racquetball

HUMAN KINETICS
The Premier Publisher for Sports & Fitness
P.O. Box 5076, Champaign, IL 61825-5076
www.HumanKinetics.com

2335